VISIBLE!

Oliver Pott

with Jan Bargfrede

VISIBLE!

Attracting Customers in a Distracted World

Translated from German
by Britta Fietzke

Campus Verlag
Frankfurt/New York

ISBN 978-3-593-51711-7 Print
ISBN 978-3-593-45391-0 E-Book (PDF)
ISBN 978-3-593-45390-3 E-Book (EPUB)

Copyright © 2023 Campus Verlag GmbH, Frankfurt am Main
Cover design: total italic, Thierry Wijnberg, Amsterdam/Berlin
Cover illustration: © iStock/Jobalou
Typesetting: Publikations Atelier, Dreieich
Printed in the United States of America

www.campus.de
www.press.uchicago.edu

Content

Invisibility equals nonexistence

We live in a visibility economy – your product or service does not exist on the market if it is invisible there. Businesses fail mostly because they do not stage their offer properly, and, thus, stay invisible to the market.

It used to be that large and expensive budgets for TV campaigns and full-page newspaper adverts were needed to gain visibility. In order to gain attention, visibility needed to be expensive, loud and shrill.

There is good news: nowadays, valuable visibility can be planned and bought with a low budget. This particularly valuable visibility is readily available as raw material, like flour for a baker.

It is smart visibility that is oftentimes quiet yet highly relevant to customers and, therefore, the basis for more customers and great success.

Businesses who have created smart visibility for their target group find new customers more easily and have a higher turnover. They are more crisis-proof and have an unbeatable edge over their competitors. Furthermore, they can scale their turnover and grow both quickly and sustainably, while building their own "brand" at the same time.

Thus, smart visibility is the solution to an urgent problem most businesses face: their own product, in which they put a lot of trust and hope, does not seem to attract the necessary attention from customers. The creation of visibility and finding of new customers is also a great challenge for companies or entrepreneurs still planning their own product manufacturing process.

The high value of smart visibility

Digitization has led to a change of perspective: it no longer depends on the range of your visibility, i.e. the number of eyes seeing you, rather, quality, value-added visibility for your defined target group has become of utter importance. And that is regardless of whether you are a doctor, lawyer, therapist or coach offering your knowledge or whether you want to market a physical product.

You are a highly specialized accountant or knee surgeon? Well, of course you could join *I'm a Celebrity … Get Me Out of Here!* if you so choose, and it would give you visibility toward an audience of millions of viewers. Yet, that is obviously not a good, value-added form of visibility – might even be toxic visibility that does more harm than good. It would not lead to more customers and a higher turnover, that is for sure, and such an appearance would not pay into your brand.

The first impression counts – and can seldomly be corrected

Visibility of your person, your brand, your product or your service stands at the beginning of any turnover. It is the first step of your marketing – as long as marketing outlines everything that motivates your customers to buy. Be it on a booth at a fair, an ad in a periodical, on the television or online, your visibility is always your earliest contact point with your customers.

These are, without fail, people who decide on what to buy or not to buy, so keep in mind: your first impression is the most important one – and there is no redoing of this first impression! Research on marketing has recognized for quite a while now that this first impression is especially embedded in people's heads, thus, they coined this magical moment the "primacy effect."[1]

You might know this yourself: you judge within seconds whether you find someone agreeable or disagreeable. To counteract this first impression takes massive amounts of effort and relationship work.

Unfortunately, this can lead to errors of judgment – maybe the other person just had a bad day, a headache or had just heard bad news? These biases of early visibility have been researched a lot and are called "halo effect"[2]: for instance, Alexander, an attractive well-spoken young man with good manners, will get better grades for the same performance than someone called Kevin, who talks with a heavy accent. The examiner is prone to transfer visible signs to the actual performance – which is, of course, objectionable.

People with glasses are considered more intelligent and literate – also a fallacy. French perfume or Italian shoes are automatically considered more exclusive, even when they were produced in a massive factory. And products in expensive and especially luxurious packaging can be sold with higher prices. The customer automatically transfers the first impression of expensive packaging on the shelf to the product itself.

Yes, that is unfair and, with a closer look, also objectionable. Customers, though, judge just as simply and reduce you and your product to the first impression of your visibility.

Companies who keep their first impression in check and build it up with much quality can control the first and most important impression on the customer. The best tool for this is visibility, which should be controlled with the mentioned three dimensions – a major part of this book.

A company with smart visibility and an immaculate first impression has a large lead in the selling process to their competitors.

Do not let your visibility roam freely!

Be aware: you are still visible to your customers on the market, whether you have or you have not actively dealt with your visibility.

You are never invisible, you just do not control your visibility.

Take large hotel review sites, for instance. They list pretty much every single hotel on the globe, and guests can review their experiences there – whether owners like this or not. There are also Internet platforms with lists of doctors, while patients write reviews and critique – even if the doctors have not added a profile themselves. On Amazon, customers will review your product and discuss it on online message boards.

And someone googling your business will find Google's star rating of one to five. A product can, if it has received a two-star rating on Amazon or Google, end up as an absolute nonstarter only days after its initial launch.

Online, employees rate their employers, so if someone looks for a certain company, these job-rating portals, due to their search engine algorithm, will be quite high on the list of results and, thanks to the halo effect, guide people's first impressions.

All of this is uncontrolled visibility with a large impact on your turnover and also, in the context of shortage of skilled workers, on the quality of your staff.

Without a proper strategy on how to control it, you hand over your visibility and with it a powerful tool to the market which will then take over the reigns. This can lead to utter chaos and to serious economic problems. Worst case scenario, this leads to a spiral of negativity through customer reviews, a "shit storm," that you will never be able to reel back in.

The main goal of smart visibility is to gain better customers and reach better turnovers. Yet, there is also a hidden, pleasant side effect, a built-in "insurance," so to speak: smart visibility prevents a bad reputation as it builds up a solid and positive image of your impression during the good days. This saves you and your company's reputation from possible crises in rougher times.

Be visible – and find the best customers and make more sales

All service providers and sellers of products want to introduce their business models to customers. And this is also where the problems start: it costs a lot of energy and has the potential for much frustration to sell a product or, even worse, develop a product to then sell to customers, and to find functioning distribution channels. There are forms of visibility with more and with less added value – yet, worse than being badly visible is being invisible.

For entrepreneurs, it is also not helpful that product development often cannot take place with the secure knowledge of having a lucrative market for it later. Finally, and maybe today more than ever, the feeling that one's own offer meets too many competitors in the struggle for the attention of potential customers, a struggle enhanced by digitalization and the fragmentation of many markets, combined with a fear that one's own piece of the cake of visibility, thus of the market, can hardly be won.

Customers are confronted with so much simultaneous information and offers that the visibility for single offers is reduced to nearly nought here as well. It seems almost impossible to become visible because too many fight over the same piece of cake.

For instance, you have worked hard on acquiring a good expertise in one special field. You can now solve problems for customers fast and with remarkable efficiency. Your are completely wrapped up in this part of your actual scope of duties, this is your true core skill. Now, you are considering leaving your employer or specializing in this area of interest with your own business.

Yet, the thought that it might not be quite easy to find yourself customers creeps up on you as there are too many competitors in your niche or market who have something similar to offer already. You might feel it in your gut that your competitors are not better than you, you might even be much better than them – still, no one sees it but you. Furthermore, your competitors have already established themselves in the market, made themselves visible.

Companies quickly and often feel like they are trying to paint the lily, like they will never be visible and will never stand a chance against all the competitors – even though they might have the better product or the better service. This inspires a feeling of hopelessness. Yet, if you want to sell something, you need to find your own visibility niche that you can use to your advantage. And it is this target conflict that can be solved with smart visibility: achieving visibility by itself is not the actual problem.

Visibility by itself is useless

Visibility just by itself is useless most times. This goes for the digital realm as well.

Take Arianna Renée for instance: she is highly visible and has gotten herself a large piece of the cake in her niche. Known as @Arii on Instagram, her account has over 2.6 million followers. All these people follow her because they want to be entertained quickly, want to be distracted or get information from her. This might lead one to the intuitive conclusion that it should be fairly easy for @Arii to get information on certain products across to her followers, in order to then use her guidance function to encourage them to buy said product. Yet, Renée is also known for the fact that she has not been able to use her fame and visibility for this exact purpose.

Certainly to commercialize her visibility with her target audience, she tried selling off-the-shelf shirts of a brand that was created for this. Yet, the production company had one single, seemingly negligible condition before starting the production process: Renée needed to sell 36 shirts in a presale. These would cover the initial costs of production and the Internet star could prove her realistic chances on the market. With over two million followers, this sounded lake a doable task to even Arianna Renée. Albeit, the unimaginable happened: she did *not* manage to sell those 36 shirts in a presale. Production never began and Renée declared later, quite ruefully, that she learned one thing from this experience: she needed to work harder.[1]

She is visible – yet, uselessly visible.

However, the reasons for her failure can be described, indeed, even seen from a positive side and are to a large extent due to an inflation of visibility in this medium: Instagram inflates visibility – just like any other successful channel with high growth rates and a lot of corporate advertisement.

While the early Internet, after leaving the first research labs, was a unidirectional medium for a long time, like the so-called "old media" (newspaper, books, television, cinema and radio), where institutionalized senders always delivered information to many receivers. Over the years, however, it changed into a new model that became part of the reason for today's Internet: it made former receivers into senders, and everyone could spread their information via the web. And everyone has been sending ever since.

It all began with blogs and the growing chances of publishing one's own contents through the first website programming to the public at large. This way, the Internet became constantly more communicative. Facebook, Instagram, YouTube (or rather their several predecessors) made it possible for pretty much anyone to find more visibility (and more easily, too) for their own topics and about their own person. Even just the name of one of Facebook's predecessors in networks, "MySpace," makes it very clear, what everything was now all about: one's own little garden in the wide variety of visibility.

One of the direct consequences of these new possibilities can be found in the now 1.2 billion active Instagram users, trying to make their own content visible. Almost all of these users spend nearly an hour a day on it to scroll through the contents. Due to the feed, the stories and IGTV, the "discover" page and hashtags, this quickly adds up to a mass of information and content – to as much as 1.2 billion hours of sending and receiving and striving for visibility and attention, mind you, that is only Instagram. Additionally, over a billion hours of video content is being watched on YouTube on a daily basis,[2] roughly 5.8 billion searches on Google are being done daily,[3] and 1.8 billion people use Facebook on a daily basis.[4]

In short, a lot is being sent and many channels put their emphasis on one KPI (key performance indicator), "Views," on visibility. By the way, all channels count these views and make them continuously accessible to the producers of these public contents – itemized for every single post, to motivate users to generate even more views and reach. This illustrates the most important aspect: visibility. Furthermore, all users of this medium are conditioned to a sort of dependence on views, number of followers and reach: "This user has many followers, logically, they must have a very successful business. This other user gets 100,000 clicks per video, they must make a ton of money with their reach."

In regards to economic aspects, visibility succumbs to a runaway inflation. Just as currencies have a problem with banks printing too much money at times without depositing a value, visibility has a problem when there is too much of it. In terms of money, it has not been deposited in its physical sense (with gold reserves in the same amount as bills and coins). The same goes for the immense and growing amount of visibility, there might not be a deposit of sufficient attention from potential viewers.

Especially with social media and as seen from the outside, people assume visibility and business success to be synonyms, just because the users have been conditioned to a greater attention to numbers of followers and clicks by the medium, and because the true correlation between the two is incomprehensible. Users do not have access to economic evaluations of the ROI for the followers of channels they are also following. Thus, it is tempting to assume that someone with many followers has an equally successful business.

Yet, this assumption based on the numbers of a large company's or successful knowledge worker's Instagram account is nothing more than idle speculation.

The inflation of visibility

So, visibility is excessively available. This is true not only for Instagram but also for other medial channels and contexts, where visibility is now more easily available and with greater capacity. When we talk of a visibility economy, it is one of the easiest economic correlations that also turned into a problem for Arianna Renée: the correlation between supply and value as a result of demand. The easier a product like visibility can be procured, the lower its value is – especially with ever more suppliers involved. This correlation is called inflation.

A large supply also has a direct influence on demand. With mobile Facebook feeds, for instance, 1.7 seconds of attention were recorded per post per user. This means that a product on offer, like the shirt offered by Arianna Renée, gets exactly this on average from every single user.[5] However, this is an insufficient amount of time to generate in the viewer an impulse to buy.

Yet, it is an advantage that visibility is so easily found nowadays. This simple access makes it more pleasant, more predictable and thus also more profitable for companies to procure this raw material. About 30 years ago, only picture editors, TV hosts and bestselling authors could attract the attention of millions of people, whereas nowadays, visibility can be bought on a schedule from Instagram, Google and Facebook.

On the downside, it has become more difficult to turn the usage of visibility as a raw material into direct profits, which was obviously part of the problem for Arianna Renée. Falling prices are more pleasant for consumers and buyers than for sellers and suppliers.

For example, a processing of gold as an expensive raw material into jewelry allows for a high value, also in the marketing of the resulting products. Yet, gold must also be bought at a high price – one of the reasons for high prices of processed gold: even the simplest and plainest processed piece of jewelry still has its gold value in resale, just because gold as a raw material is rare and correspondingly valuable.

If, however, someone were to start selling a cheap machine tomorrow with which every household could extract a few kilos of gold per day from tap water, then that would devalue all already available gold. Neither the gold nor, for that matter, the machine filtering it would be worth anything after a while, at least not after the commodity gold had flooded the market. To the same extent, visibility and its filtering machines have been devalued by the Internet. As a direct consequence, the use of visibility as a raw material can no longer generate any immediate value if it is kept unrefined.

The large amount of visibility that is available to successful Instagrammers is also (at least theoretically) available to all others, which many use in their favor already. Furthermore, now it is not just one single individual or institution producing content while the rest of the world consumes: every consumer is now also a producer, thus a mix of producer and consumer, of sender and receiver. All users are also senders, while receiving from many other senders. Every single message is now part of a white noise of billions and billions of messages – and is in danger of disappearing.

Arianna Renée really needs to think on what she wants to "work harder" on, as the production of even more worthless visibility will not help her much.

"Loud" visibility obliterates the market's appreciation for you

By the way, the "old media" are also familiar with this phenomenon. A product being shown in a popular evening program reached millions of viewers – with nearly no other competing products nearby, thus it had extraordinary visibility.

With the occurrence of private channels and broadcasts, which also had far more lax regulations on their advertisements, visibility of television advertisement became inflationary. TV ads and single products met with more and more competition on the same channels. For instance, detergent now vied for consumers on television, not just on the shelves. Previously, customers used to decide in the shop on which product to buy – however, television advertisement changed all that, as the decision to buy was now mostly made in the living room based on television coverage. This turned visibility into the first and foremost piece of marketing.

Adverts became more creative, colorful and, ultimately, insistent. Ads for detergent previously praised its "good quality," while they now promised the "whitest of white." And just a few years later, consumers were being shouted at from television ads with "Tight is right!" or "I'm not that stupid!"[6] This is loud visibility, not smart visibility.

Even though, an escalation of this was driven further, it now feels like this concept is petering out slowly. First of all, this form of advertisement on television has taken a backseat. Besides, television advertisements – just like ads on the radio, in newspapers and cinemas, just generally in the old media – have apparently passed their prime. Ad revenue has been declining for years, a trend that coincided with the emergence of the social web.

Nowadays, simple visibility has long transgressed its peak of intrinsic value as the basis for lucrative business models. It has been proven more often than not that the idea of making revenue just from visibility is a fallacy. And even frantic tries to attain even more visibility or become even louder have failed. That is a phenomenon we are all too familiar with in our own private lives: there is always someone at a party trying to tell a story, speaking loudly and gesticulating wildly. They literally fight for attention – while it becomes more and more arduous and unsatisfying to listen to them.

Yet, there are also charismatic people everyone likes to listen to, even when they are being quiet. They have relevant topics to talk about, they seem to be on the same wavelength as us and we could literally hear a pin drop because everyone is hanging onto their every word. Other people seem to be drawn to these people – *because* they are not loud. They reach an interesting form of visibility and build a special connection with other people, who then strive to absorb their contents. Suddenly, a sender does not impose their visibility onto others, rather, potential receivers look for it.

This sort of visibility is what we are striving for because it is quieter and not imposed on others through sheer quantity and noise. This we call smart visibility – it is sought-after, unobtrusive, lives off its own charisma and its connection to the sender. This is by far the more intelligent way for most companies to reach their customers and visibility that sticks out on all levels. And it also, once again, is valuable.

The era of visibility empires is at an end

Not too long ago, visibility was concentrated on a few handful of beacons of bright light. In his book *White*,[7] the bestselling author Bret Easton Ellis describes the spirit of our time, our *zeitgeist*, as an era in which the visibility empires have perished. There used to be rock bands whose newest albums were awaited eagerly and who got massive attention from the media, thus, visibility. They were invited to large chat shows to talk about their newest album and received the highest visibility possible.

Films used to have the same effect: every new *James Bond* still gets this sort of media attention before and after publication. The same empires are still discernible in the market of fiction – certain authors, like the French Michel Houellebecq or the US-American Ken Follett, still receive a lot of attention from media, with book reviews being published in large newspapers. For instance, each of the former's last six books have reached bestselling status right after publication in German-speaking countries.

These "empires" still live on their momentum, which they bring with them from their own history and strong brand. Take Abba's new album *Voyage*, for instance, which has only received the greatest possible media attention because Abba still feeds off the nimbus of their own empire – despite the fact they broke up in 1982 (more than 40 years ago), and have hardly been visible as a band with new projects since.

The Beatles' album *Let it be* also dates back half a century and again received the greatest media attention on the occasion of its anniversary. In a multi-part Disney series, Paul McCartney talked about the album's genesis, while also publishing a biography of his own favorite songs. The album also appeared in a new edition and was massively marketed – it received all this attention even though it is already 50 years old. Thus, *Let it be* has retained its visibility over the course of many years, and has resurrected said visibility like the anniversary's crystallization seed which, seemingly, had never faded.

Later on, we will show how good storytelling can help preserve this visibility over longer periods of time.

Even the new *James Bond* is always highly anticipated by the public because the film series has become something of an institution. And take Michel Houellebecq again, who has been fancied as a candidate for the Nobel Prize of Literature for decades. Moreover, he claimed after the publishing of his latest novel, *Anéantir* (French for "destroy"), that it would also be his last – once again leading to large publicity and visibility, which will probably have been quite advantageous for its sales numbers.

These monuments of visibility have become rare in numbers and are done by now: do you remember a similarly large staging for a new film hitting the cinemas? (Apart from the *Marvel* franchise?) Yes, they still exist, these long-awaited cinema films, take *Matrix 4 Resurrections*, for instance – but they have become rare, and when they are highly anticipated, than that is due to their history. As with the *Matrix* series, whose first epic and genre-defining part came out in 1999, the last century, nonetheless. Only based on this foundation of a decades-old visibility did the sequel receive so much attention.

Yet, most of the new cinema films receive little to no attention, even if they are especially expensive blockbusters with famous actors and actresses.

Such a visibility erosion is also discernible in the music business and is most probably the reason why nearly all musicians cannot live off their music alone anymore. Not too long ago, a musician's performance on a large TV show would lead to a large visibility of millions of viewers, which would then without a doubt translate directly into record sales. Visibility was directly linked to revenue, which then led to a faithful fan base for musicians. Out of self-interest, the major labels would arrange for more coverage and visibility.

"Be visible first, earn money later," was the official rule of thumb.

Nowadays, it is the other way around: only the visible ones can build up on this success, will be invited to TV shows – and can earn money.

"To get a truly profitable record deal with a major label, bands or solo artists need an already existent fan base," explains Hubert Wandjo, head of Music and Creative Industries Department at the German Pop Academy in Mannheim.[8] He now advises young artists who have not yet been able to generate their own visibility to rather set up their own label, thus following a DIY approach.

The basic idea is obvious: previously, the product itself was sufficiently attention-grabbing and there were attractive public channels for the presentation of a product to a large audience, thus, creating visibility. The product more or less sold itself, and quite effortlessly, too. Today, visibility toward a target group needs to be built up first – and only then can it be turned into sales.

Visibility does not disappear – it is split up

What happened to the audience? One could assume that the viewers' attention has disappeared and faded. A fallacy.

Reasons for visibility erosion are numerous and different, yet, they are all based on the breaking apart of previously great names, products and institutions into much smaller elements. Now, the associated niche visibility is accessible to everyone, as the high entry barriers have fallen. This makes visibility more easily available and turns it into a more democratic process – that is the first very good news for you because now you no longer need an empire to draw attention to your cause.

In the past, a feature film could only be produced by one of the large studios, like Warner Brothers, Universal or Disney, partly because the necessary production technology was unaffordable, while channels to reach consumers were equally guarded and expensive: airtime on big TV stations for commercials, for example, or the huge expense of getting a film into cinemas. Additionally, big Hollywood stars tried getting the focus on their own visibility and, since they could juice up any film with their charisma, demanded exorbitant fees. Therefore, only the big film companies could afford blockbuster productions.

Today, a simple film can be recorded with just an iPhone camera, and it can also be edited directly on the same device – certainly, the final product's quality cannot be compared to a cinema production, but it has a much better price-result ratio, by a long shot. Later parts of this book will show in particular that just the technical quality is no longer a success factor if the content's quality is good enough, and if the viewer is extensively linked to the new visibility channels. Also, the low-tech video can be made directly accessible to millions of viewers without guarded access, making it up-to-the-minute, direct and fast.

YouTube, Instagram, Facebook and TikTok have now more reach than any of the large television channels, and they are not guarded by expensive access hurdles like these channels or cinemas.

Yet, why did this fragmentation happen in the first place, and why do we find ourselves amidst a zeitgeist that merges sender and receiver into a "prosumer"? The reasons are essentially rooted in the so-called "Long-Tail theory," which has been dealing with this matter since the Internet's early days.[9]

This approach claims that big stars, shows and products were accepted simply because there was no alternative. Take Germany for instance, until the mid-1980s – well before the advent of commercial Internet usage –, three TV stations were available in each German federal state: ARD, ZDF and the respective regional program, the so-called "Dritte" (literally, the "third"). Viewers could only choose one of these programs at a time, and for lack of an alternative, certain programs like *Wetten, dass …?*[10] became popular. They covered as wide an audience as possible, thus, these shows were just as compatible with 10-year-old schoolchildren as with people over 75.

At the same time, they had to be a compromise. Special interests or narrowcasts were not envisaged and also impossible due to the tailoring to such a wide audience. Those were then either fringe programs or later niche channels. This meant that television to a large extent had a relevance problem as a medium: if one part of a program on a Saturday night was uninteresting, like a bet on *Wetten dass …?* or a music gig, the audience had to endure this part, hoping that the next part with another emphasis or topic might be more interesting.

This changed with the emergence of private television channels. Now, with double the number of channels, there was a larger broadcasting variety and the number of viewers spread across twice as many channels. This lead to lower viewing figures for each channel – thus, directly impacting on each channel's visibility. For the first time, viewers had more alternatives; with cable and satellite connections, hundreds of niche channels were now available. With each new niche channel, reach was further reduced, while, at the same time, each channel's relevance increased.

Then the Internet, as for instance YouTube, overhauled the landscape of moving images, mainly for the following reasons:

- The number of (YouTube) channels was now nearly endless, which made them highly relevant. Those interested in polo or orchids would generally not find anything of relevance to them on standard channels. With YouTube, viewers can put together their own program with different contents.
- Moving images broke away from broadcast synchronicity: when a program on TV was on at an inopportune time, for example during working hours, or if two programs overlapped, viewers had to choose. This rather important disadvantage just does not exist for asynchronous broadcasting forms like YouTube channels.
- At the same time, visibility became mobile – whereas previously, TV channels could only be watched in the living room or bedroom at home, YouTube channels can be watched anywhere and everywhere, as long as a smartphone is available.
- There is more interactive engagement with users with Internet visibility: they can comment, ask questions or forward a video to friends who might be interested.
- Concurrently – and this is sometimes overlooked or at least undervalued – the purchase chain was streamlined by the convergence of e-commerce with the visibility channel. For the first time, visibility could directly, and measurably, be linked to sales. Previously, only the viewing rate could be measured, thus, only the reach of visibility generated for one product in an ad. The customer was expected to make a media break for the purchase; they had to buy a product later on in a shop, or, more rarely (but better), a product could be ordered directly via phone. With Internet, the situation changed: direct purchase links can be included in video clips, thus, the purchase is made immediately on the same device on which the video is running – visibility can convert into purchase impulses and into sales right away.

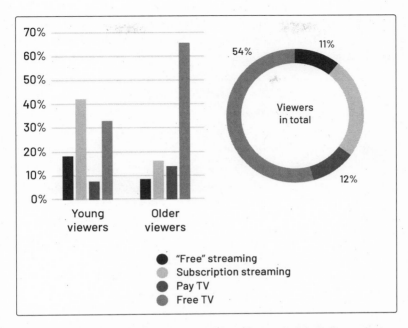

Allocation of viewing time in Germany: traditional linear television is increasingly losing viewers, especially younger viewers (ages 16–29). For them, above all else, program channels have one aspect in common: irrelevance.

Source: original illustration, after a statistic by Roland Berger[11]

For the long-tail approach, television is one of the more obvious examples, but the collapse of former empires can be witnessed in almost every area of visibility in the public sphere. For instance, previously – due to the limited number of available shelves – only a few performers and artists could be found in music stores. While nowadays and mostly thanks to Spotify, an unlimited number of ambitious artists can tap into an audience.

Here, too, the pattern is discernible: previous superstars had to be versatile and attractive to a large number of listeners, otherwise they just would not be signed with a major label, leaving their work largely invisible. The problem with superstars: listeners had to compromise with them, too. That was until Spotify created a platform for an almost infinite number of new artists: now fans no longer had to compromise – they found things exactly to their taste, even if that meant that a song might only have a few hundred listeners.

The cake is now being divided into many smaller pieces. For example, in 1984, 55,000 new songs were published – while the same number of new songs is being published on the Internet every single day.[12] Due to this high degree of fragmentation, an extremely large proportion of these songs remains invisible – which also explains why the majority of artists cannot establish a meaningful economic concept from this.

Large cinema productions have also had to face considerable competition. With their Hollywood superstars, they were once a guarantee for greatest visibility. They still exist today and Quentin Tarantino's newest film would still garner wide media attention. At the same time, however, numerous series are a worthy competition now, some of which with very high-quality and lavish productions, from streaming providers such as Netflix, Amazon Prime, Disney or Sky.

They started off as visibility channels for existing cinema productions but have now developed into content production companies and film studios. Their variety of different series is now sheer unmanageable, while, at the same time, their actors are often only known to fans and disappear into oblivion after the series has ended. Thus, productions of new series are much cheaper than that of Hollywood films because now production technology is cheaper and the actors can demand far less money.

The series' success factor from the customers' point of view is now more pertinent: while a major feature film has to be compatible with a much larger audience, which, for instance, leads a *James Bond* to having to walk the (well, rather contrived) tightrope between a love story and an action film, while a special-interest series can concentrate on a single genre and therefore satisfy the audience's needs much better.

However, the decline in visibility of once great product empires is also evident with physical goods. The *Dr. Oetker-Backbuch* ("baking book"), for example, was an institution in German-speaking countries for decades with a more than a century long history – including its own school cookbook, which has been sold over 19 million times since 1911 and is, according to the publisher, the most successful baking book in the world.[13] The book includes cooking recipes on almost 600 pages.

This pillar of the food-processing corporation Dr. Oetker, which ensured on-point visibility with the perfect target group in pretty much every German kitchen, has now faced considerable competition: mostly due to online bookselling, niche recipe books can now be published in smaller editions; self-publishing even allows for micro-niche recipe books with providers such as the German BoD or epubli, who provide print on demand so that a book is only printed after it has been ordered by a customer.

Yet, recipes can no longer only be found in books: a large number are available on YouTube channels, on Instagram, in cooking shows and as recipe apps. And if you feel like baking a lemon cake, you might now look up the recipe online instead of in Dr. Oetker's baking book. The visibility of the former Oetker book empire is fragmented into numerous channels.

These sometimes rather unusual recipes are highly relevant to the target group: if you were, for instance, looking for both vegan and gluten-free recipes, a classic cookbook would not be a good option for you, though it was more compatible with the masses than a specialist offer.

So all in all, customers are not necessarily consuming fewer recipes, the market has just fragmented into many more recipe channels.

Customers demand more

Due to the long-tail process, the customer gets a more fitting, relevant and connectable product, previously unreachable by a blockbuster offer – a higher, more uncompromising quality for customers, which increases their expectations of both the product's content and all levels of product experience.

Today's discerning consumers want to be a part of entire product worlds: a simple filter coffee has become insufficient, as people can choose between a variety of coffee specialities, prepared at home with capsules, or the carefully and extremely elaborately staged world of Starbucks coffee, where they not only get a freshly prepared chai latte with their own name on the cup but also a feel-good world surrounding them. A filter coffee can do nothing like that – as a result, Starbucks can charge formidable prices. Again, later parts of this book deal intensively with the resulting market opportunity of enhancing visibility through storytelling.

The much courted customer now rejects their role as a mere recipient of promotional visibility; they have learned to expect a personal coffee, even labeled with their own name.

This attitude of entitlement was first encountered in the online world: customers (unconsciously) found out that visibility functions on two levels, and that they could comment, like and rate posts. They became the protagonist of the product universe and were given a voice. On Amazon, for example, it is no longer sufficient to just offer a product because customers will not only review the product but will probably also share it with their friends – whether the manufacturer wants them to or not. They can also make their displeasure seen and heard in company support forums or on the company's Instagram or Facebook pages.

They can rate their favorite Netflix series with stars directly in the app or even leave a comment. This prompt and direct customer testimony means that some streaming providers no longer produce finished series but instead first produce and broadcast a pilot episode. If this then fails the company's KPIs (for example, average viewer retention, measured by viewing time or premature film termination, or comments, ratings), the whole series is not only discontinued but does not even get produced beyond the pilot episode.

In this regard, traditional cinema and linear TV are lagging behind: expensive feature films have to be produced in their entirety, and teams have to hope that it will reach the audience. Then and only then can box office turnovers in the cinema be ascertained – it becomes clear much too late whether a film is profitable. The linear channel of old media is reduced to one-dimensional communication with customers, thus (at least partly) missing early indicators such as premature viewing abandonment.

The time of famous and aloof film stars, whom the audience could at most marvel at on a film festival's or premiere's red carpet, seems to be largely over. At best, series fans feel connected to the stars. Something similar is happening in the music business. In a very personal article, multi-platinum superstar Jennifer Paige ("Crush") reported on her fall from internationally celebrated superstar to an indie artist who had to scrape together the money for her latest album with a crowdfunding campaign: "I grew up with a music industry in which the artists' enigma was their biggest allure."[14]

The new artist generation is either known to a niche audience at best or, if there are still superstars among them, they show themselves to be much more open to fans and, in doing so, also tap into new sources of revenue. The German daily news service *Tagesschau*, for example, reported on the billion-dollar business of K-pop:

"There are many ways to get close to the 'idols' – as K-pop stars are called – through livestreams, TV appearances and interviews," explains K-pop fan Ndugwa. Paid apps upload "behind the scenes" videos, fans can arrange to have virtual lunches with their idols or ask them questions about their personal lives. "The digital networking with fans and the participatory nature are a major factor for the success of K-pop bands. This creates a pseudo-intimacy," as musicologist Fuhr points out. "There are even special audio recordings where band members whisper to help their fans fall asleep." Ndugwa finishes with the remark that the market was huge.[15]

The culture of flat fees: the devaluation of contents

This fragmentation of visibility has significant consequences for those who have previously made money from content. There is a growing flat fee culture in which content is played out for the lowest possible fees.

A Spotify subscription, for example, is available for a small monthly fee; a Netflix subscription with hundreds of high-quality series costs about as much as one, maybe two, visits to the cinema. Formerly expensive high-quality video coaching courses are now available on YouTube for free. And the software segment has also been hit by inflation: just a few years ago, large purchase money could be gotten for high-quality graphics or accounting applications. Nowadays, apps – often disruptive and easy to use – by young start-ups are available for small amounts.

However, this inflation of content can also be an opportunity for the visibility of channels, as this book will show.

"Snack Content" – attention span of a goldfish

This inflation of even good, high-quality content has made the audience more demanding and also more impatient. Those used to spending 400 euros on a complex graphics program are more patient when it comes to learning new functions, than people generally are with a free app: if the usage of the graphics app, the test version of which was previously downloaded free of charge, is not intuitive and immediately usable, it gets deleted – after all, several alternatives are available.

Spotify songs are also becoming shorter and more concise: while CD or vinyl fans regard the product more patiently, if only because they bought it and now expect a benefit, Spotify's music flat fee means that the next song is only a click away if it is not immediately liked, or only very short sequences of a few seconds from a song are listened to repeatedly because the attention span does not allow for more.

The German weekly newspaper *DIE ZEIT* writes about this trend with a sarcastic undertone: "Today, parents suffer more than ever: they are allowed to listen to a song's same 15 seconds over and over again when their children are on TikTok while sitting next to them. There, clip after clip, challenge after challenge, regurgitating the same song fragments over and over. Not only does this grate on these parents' nerves, it also changes the creation of pop music – and what makes a song a hit."[16]

Here, too, it is an inflation of content, devaluing it in the process, so that artists can hardly expect any significant income from licensing revenues. Visibility is extremely fragmented and taken out of context. The quote given above also indicates that these 15 seconds of briefest attention decide on what becomes a hit – this has significant consequences for visibility campaigns, which must be strategically planned and considered accordingly.

Something similar goes for Readly, a Swedish platform offering many magazines, even internationally, for a flat fee, or Amazon Kindle Unlimited, where books can be downloaded and read for a monthly fee.

This inflation of content is exacerbated by an inflation of available individual screens. Once, there was a single television in the living room, but now there is a large number of other screens in households: smartphones, book readers like the Amazon Kindle, iPads, notebooks. Today, the use of a second screen while watching a TV show or a Netflix series is more than common, and to use it to further research information or exchange WhatsApp messages ("multi-screens"). Obviously, this significantly reduces the attention on one piece of content, so much so that watching films or series has become the sidekick, not the main event. The high image density and the editing speed of individual scenes is also a result of the reduced attention span.

A team of researchers from the Max Planck Institute for Human Development is dedicated to this topic and investigated the reduction of attention spans. The main research focus was the question of how long a blockbuster film or book bestseller, a social media topic or other content was in the public eye, having great visibility. For this purpose, the team compiled data on cinema attendance from the last 40 years and book sales figures from the last 100 years.

The result: they could prove that the average attention span has been reduced considerably. Twitter hashtags, which focus on a (popular) topic or event, are exemplary for this trend: in 2013, a relevant Twitter hashtag used to be in the top 50 for 17.5 hours, thus, very visible; only three years later, though, this had been reduced to 11.9 hours.

Similar ramifications can be seen with Hollywood blockbusters and best-selling books, which, formerly, were global, enduring visibility monuments. "Our data shows that the duration during which the public shows interest in individual topics and content is constantly becoming shorter. At the same time, interest changes ever faster from one topic to the next," reports Philipp Lorenz-Spreen, the study's author at the Max Planck Institute.[17]

That is the reason why today's contents are being called "snack content" – they need to be easily digestible without being, unfortunately, too sustainable, nutrition-wise, so to speak, just like chocolate bars.

A much-noticed Microsoft study also comes to a frightening conclusion, which has even made it onto the frontpage of mass media with headlines such as "Attention span of a goldfish." The core message being that the average human viewer's online attention is now below that of a goldfish.

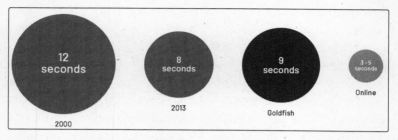

The results of Microsoft's research paper: the first two circles depict the average human attention span in 2000 and 2013. That of a goldfish is 9 seconds; while online, human attention span is only somewhere between 3 to 5 seconds.

Source: original illustration according to the data from the Microsoft Research Report[18]

However, data carriers – the medium on which content reaches consumers – also significantly determine the attention span for individual tracks. The CD, for instance, can hold 78 minutes of music, which also defined the length of individual songs. Radio stations prefer to broadcast three minute long songs, which enables them to place a sufficient number of ads – also the reason why this is a typical duration of a piece of music.

And what about today? Spotify, in particular, due to its dominant position in the music industry, is the defining factor now. For the company to pay out royalties, a song needs to have been played for at least 30 seconds; yet, longer durations do not equal higher payments to artists. So, from a business point of view, it makes sense to produce as many short songs as possible. Market professionals predict for the next ten years, that song lengths could be down to only one minute for a piece of music.[19]

This trend is also discernible in the film industry: while a film for traditional cinema still lasts about 90 minutes, series produced for the streaming today are divided into short episodes of 20 to 40 minutes.

This has immediate and significant consequences for your own digital visibility: you have to get straight to the point, but when you do not – specifically in the first 5 seconds of online attention span – generate enough momentum to encourage the viewer to continue watching, even the best visibility campaign is doomed to fail.

Good news though: if you strategically address your visibility and play out relevant content you can expect very high attention spans. Later on, we will deal with examples of YouTube videos that viewers can easily watch for an hour, that are highly anticipated by audiences and garner widespread attention within minutes of their release.

Establish visibility for that which is being sought after – and make sure that you are being found

Although visibility is losing value, at least in its purest sense as broad visibility, companies cannot survive without it. Still, it is the only way to gain access to potential consumers of products or contents, which only then makes it a suitable business model. However, visibility must be refined to circumvent the short attention span of viewers with this inflationary raw material.

Only visibility reveals new market opportunities. To understand how to turn visibility into a business model, precisely this connection is worth a closer look. If certain forms of visibility do not generate market opportunities, or if companies feel too great a lack of opportunities to turn visibility into a business model, the focus then needs to change to market opportunities and their creation even without visibility.

Economic studies[20] describe the concept of "market opportunity" as follows: it is created in the overlap between a company's abilities, which are then translated into a service or product, and the customers' needs that the company seeks to satisfy in the market. As a result, companies with products that meet customer needs have an opportunity in the market.

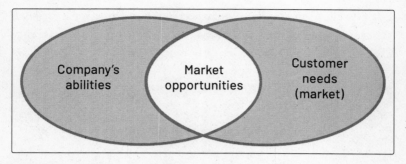

Market opportunities arise between the company's abilities and the customers' needs.

Source: original illustration

Yet, in terms of entrepreneurial success, this is half the truth at most be-cause, up to this point, it is no more than a vague chance. And as is the case with football, not the team that creates more chances wins but the one that scores more goals.

According to the model, the market opportunity happens at the over-lap between customer needs and a company's abilities and products. The more the two overlap, the better the opportunity. Therefore, at least theoretically, it just needs a look at both sides and to then bring them together as closely as possible – thus, giving a company excellent mar-ket opportunities. This is just as true as it is too easy.

Still, the model offers an excellent bedrock for solving the challenge of an attainable market opportunity: a company should direct its par-ticular attention to the production of something sought after. It should also take good care of being found quickly – at best, while creating the products with the company's abilities and also while directly looking at the later overlap with customer needs.

A company's abilities

Let us first have a look at the individual elements before going into the why and how of smart visibility as a must in this model. A company's products are a translation of its abilities, of what it can achieve. Each product has properties that consequently also help determine its market opportunities. A simplified selection of which is as follows:

- **Quality** – often defined as the satisfaction of customer expectations, thereby also signifying an important connection to the customers themselves. A product can brilliantly solve a customer's problem – should the customer not have said problem, they would not buy the product.
- Consequently: **problem-solving competence**. A customer will naturally only pay for a product or a service when they assume that it will solve their problem. The problem's size and the solution's singularity are an important aspect of this, as is the solution's potential to offer the customer a shortcut to the solution.
- **Production or technical quality** – for instance, a fountain pen made by Montblanc is bought and appreciated, among other aspects, for its workmanship, and Mercedes Benz marketing claims that one should buy "Either the best or nothing at all."
- **Availability** – is the product available to customers at all, and can it be made available to all the customers who want it?
- **Integral quality** – simplified, the question of whether the customer can use the product for themselves. For instance, a customer would never buy a battery for a machine that they do not have – even with the best of performance data imaginable.[21]

> Yet, the product itself, all of its performance data and the problem-solving quality for the customer do not exist on the market as long as the product is invisible to its potential customers!

These properties are only inscribed in the product but useless and invisible without customer interaction.

The business skills are, in a sense, the tinkerer's aspect. A product that focuses very much on its technological and technical performance, while mostly ignoring the market during its development, is called an engineer-driven product. Therein, too, lies a trap for a dangerously noncustomer-centered approach to visibility. This way of developing products is as luring as it is outdated in many aspects.

German economy is based not least on the external recognition that most of its products are strongly driven by engineering. German mechanical engineering, for example, the economy's poster child, is known globally for its combination of highest precision and performance. However, a zeitgeist-driven shift toward less perfect products that can be brought to market quickly has become apparent. Today's economy has become, increasingly so, an economy of information as well as data and its structuring and bundling – an aspect that the most successful and valuable companies in the world often derive their real value from. This is as true for Apple as it is for Google and also for companies like Tesla. The latter of which, in particular, continues to amaze with nearly grotesquely high stock market values that can hardly be explained solely by superior precision and its products' technological edge. Tesla and Google, for example, bring products to market quickly, with error-tolerance, a willingness to learn and a focus on customer needs.

Yet, a constant turn of the quality screw is barely in demand today because an economy that essentially (while also creating value) trades in information and attention instead of steel and gross register tonnes of goods can create value from its raw materials much more quickly. Products now travel around the globe at lightning speed; and because we live in an age where everyone is a sender, other quality standards have become acceptable which enabled a thinking in much shorter production cycles. Put simply, precision is still a distinguishing quality feature for a machine that masters high-precision steel shaping, but a lower quality standard is sufficient for a smartphone app because the provider can update it constantly.

Customer needs

The other side of the simple equation for the description of market opportunities is: customer needs. To best understand them, they should be seen as a state of lack: customers have a problem – which can be of a negative sort, such as a headache or the need for a loan, or of the positive sort, like the client's desire for personal development or a nice children's birthday present.

Yet, something is always missing in this system; in the existing solution vacuum, the customer's need results from a desire for solutions.

The greater the customer's "minus state," i.e. the greater their problem, and the more the company's offer is in a "plus state," the easier it will be for the products and offers to find their way to the customer – thus, the desired market success! The offer's "plus state" is defined by the product features just listed. When they fit the customer's needs particularly well, then the "minus" is as large as possible which makes the sale easier.

However, analogous to the company's offers, one aspect has to be made clear here: just by themselves, customer needs are not an important factor for a business. Once again, it needs smart visibility because customers need to be able to see a company's offers, and because they want to feel that their individual needs are reflected in these products.

What is exciting here is that customer needs by themselves generate just as few market opportunities as the company's abilities alone – instead, they need to be transformed as well: into customer expectations.

While customer needs are initially undirected and only describe the customer's lack of something, customer expectations are the extrapolation and first stage of guiding these needs. Behind customer expectations is the customer's belief in their problem's solvability. We should think of it like a story of the man shipwrecked on a desert island: he will feel a certain lack, probably even several – for water and food, for company and certainly for speedy rescue. His needs are both recognizable and very pronounced, but it is only with the passing of a ship that these needs are addressed.

You may imagine the stranded man excitedly waving at the ship. Suddenly, in his expectation, the ship will soon serve his needs – by rescuing and providing. Whereas, prior to the ship's appearance, he only had a need, while now he has a precise idea of how it could be met.

Even more so, the stranded man now, in turn, tries to establish visibility toward the rescuing ship by waving or with smoke signals; and he might even try to swim to the ship to solve his problem. It is precisely this change that describes the transition from customer needs to customer expectations and – with an explicit emphasis on this – it is the ship's visibility that makes the difference here.

There are no fair market chances

It becomes truly difficult at the overlap of a company's abilities and customer needs – at least at the latest, as reality is far more complex than the model. Market opportunities are not equal, they do not simply arise between offers and needs, instead, they depend on many factors.

Cheese, for instance, is a popular and widespread product, especially in western cultures. There alone, about 5,000 different types of cheese can be found,[22] simply because many people like to eat cheese and a correspondingly large amount of cheese is bought. Furthermore, these are only the types of cheese distinguishable by definition, such as "Gouda" or "Cheddar." So far, the economic model is correct: there is a clear customer need for cheese and it is matched by suppliers with their product offer. However, there is not just one product, but there are many, many types of cheese. The abundant demand causes a highly differentiated market, many types of cheese are produced by several suppliers – slightly differently and with different characteristics.

In Germany, for instance, there are already thousands of smaller and larger cheese dairies selling their products and competing for customers with cheese from the Netherlands, Switzerland, Italy and all over the world. There are a few large suppliers who share a large part of the market among themselves, and many small ones who have to make do with marginal market shares. Yet, the question remains, is it really the customers' benevolence, i.e. the positive affinity, or is it not rather visibility that makes the difference?

Like the cheese dairies, many companies face this challenge: their product is not seen, even though they have manufactured it ambitiously as a great product.

Standing in front of the cheese display in the supermarket, there may be 20 or 30 different types of cheese from different manufacturers. Some supermarkets also like to serve the trend toward regional offers with a few regional cheeses. The majority of cheese-producing companies that would like to conquer a larger market share, however, remain invisible to potential customers in the supermarket cheese section because their own product is simply not on offer.

Do you know Anneau du Vic Bilh, for instance? You would recognize it immediately because it has an unmistakable hole in the middle of the cheese wheel, it is a Pyrenean speciality well known among connoisseurs. Or the mild goat's milk cheese Cathare de Saint-Félix Fermier?[23] Both are wonderful types of cheese for sure, but are unfortunately hardly known outside their region, while the latter is even produced in strictly limited quantities. Young Gouda, sliced, in a 250 gram pack of the supermarket-own brand, on the other hand, is known to many consumers because it is sold in abundance.

This has nothing to do with the individual cheese's quality. Cheese tenderly made by hand in small cheese dairies often lose out to industrially produced, pre-packaged cheese slices cut from meter-long cheese blocks which correspond to the average taste rather than offering an exciting new taste experience to a cheese gourmet.

Many customers would agree any time – perhaps somewhat unreflectively and possibly even incorrectly when analyzed more closely – when one claims that a small Alpine cheese dairy's cheese, produced with a sustainable milk production, for instance according to the criteria of the organic farming association "Demeter,"[24] offers higher quality than a cheese from an industrial farm with conventional milk production.

Even if industrial cheese were to achieve at least the same quality on various levels, for example microbiologically or in terms of nutritional values, the customer would still like to buy the mountain cheese: after all, it is very special! On holiday in Switzerland at the Alpine farm's show dairy, the customer ends up buying precisely this cheese – and at kilo prices that would normally be considered sheer profiteering in the supermarket. Judging by many of the characteristics of French handmade monastery cheeses, each of them should have an excellent market chance compared to an industrially produced cheese. Characteristics such as the manufacturing process, the taste with a high recognition value, the beautifully told story of the individual cheese's unique tradition as well as many more factors can definitely appeal to cheese lovers.[25]

Albeit, customers cannot find the French monastery cheese in the supermarket in Hamburg – it is simply invisible. Then, a cheese of exquisite taste, made with the best craftsmanship, is of absolutely no use to the supplier. If the cheese is invisible on the cheese display, it cannot be bought. The product quality is not the decisive factor – but also not the customer needs. And no one even heard about the company's abilities, therefore, at least in regards to this product, there is no overlap – and no market opportunity, none at all.

> If visibility were a commodity available to everyone to the same extent, all of this would look very different. It is just not the case that products or services meet existing customer needs to the same extent, and that, at this overlap, serving customer needs as best as possible would be a guarantee for an equal market opportunity, let alone for a business model. As logical and comprehensible as this may seem reading these lines, this simple connection is highly treacherous when not explicitly stated.

Many product developers secretly believe that they only need to go through production of high-quality products to then be able to sell to customers.

By the way, there is a little test algorithm to see whether you yourself are susceptible to this seductive way of thinking: have you been developing a service or product for a long time but are still improving and increasing the quality before finally going on to the sales bit? You may already be putting visibility behind perfection, thus, preventing your own success.

Market chances alone are useless

Back to the market chance to then turn it into a practical participation in the market.

Even when only two companies' products meet customer needs in a market, competitive advantages and product differences, as well as prices, branding and dozens of other factors, mean shifts in each company's market opportunity – to the other's disadvantage.

This problem is only nonexistent in monopolistic markets – albeit, they are rarely conquered. In all other cases, it is always about which product the customer sees more often and better.

Nevertheless, suppliers often give only second thoughts to the product's need for visibility toward the customer – including all its features and qualities. To be blunt, this minimizes the product's chances. Suppliers tinker and develop instead of thinking about what is perhaps the most important aspect: which part of my offer will be visible later, and how? Particularly high-performance surfactants or the benefits they bring?

For many products, a consistent focus on customer needs as well as the customer's view of the product and its problem-solving offers is a lever for the so-called Product-Market Fit: the moment a product meets real demand in the market.

> Instead, it must be seen the other way around: to have the best product which clearly meets customer needs but does not gain visibility is like waving to the searching customers in the dark.

In consequence, this means that if, for instance, suppliers experience a mismatch between their product's tested and experienced quality (also compared to the competition) and their customers' demand, then visibility might be the key to finding the reason. And vice versa, a smart use of visibility can be *the* competitive edge par excellence.

Visibility is the first step to actual sales

So there are still important factors missing from both the figure below and the idea it conveys of the intersection of a company's abilities as well as customer needs in order to turn market opportunities into sales.

The importance of visibility for companies, which makes *the* difference on the cheese display, denotes this gap. Thus, visibility as a decisive factor for a service provider's or product supplier's market opportunities is the path through all other challenges a company has to face between the production and sales. A company *can* in principal (and to varying degrees) solve all challenges concerning a sale to a customer, the quality, the price, the solution offered and the customer's benefit, the solution's side effects or the question of the customer's trust in the product; yet, it almost always *has to* show them!

This means that visibility must replace market opportunity in the model. Then, market opportunity emerges from a smartly managed visibility that facilitates between a company's abilities and customer needs in the market.

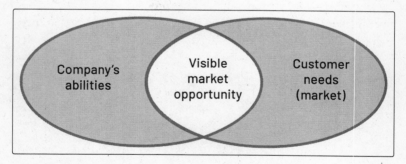

Only the visible market opportunity links a company's abilities to customer needs in the real market. Otherwise, a (theoretical) market opportunity occurs but is unseen by the customer.

Source: original illustration

Marketing has become more honest

There are excellent visibility specialists: a company's marketing department. Whether the company owner is self-employed, or whether a company has a whole department of marketers: they are the ones who ultimately create visibility for the company and translate it into sales.

Technicians and engineers develop the technical product, while it is the marketing department's task to advertise it.

In the past and particularly with engineering-driven corporate products, it felt like a company's creative people were the ones who ended up tying the funny bows around products for the shipment to customers. While the marketing department was just a group of people sitting around at their desks, been given a football table so that they would not disturb the engineers doing their important work.

As a correct cog in the machine, marketing later describes the made product; unfortunately, in terms of content, this creates a certain distance between a product and its marketing. Now, not only the marketing department feels like it is not close enough to the actual product and its development – customers, too, get the feeling that big words are being used in marketing for something they can either believe or, well, not. This is called "overpromising" – promising more than the product can actually deliver.

As a long-term consequence, it seems paradoxical to customers to have the words "advertising" and "honest" in the same sentence. Advertising is certainly not perceived as honest by every customer or every viewer. Furthermore, if there is more and more advertising on more and more channels, it seems counterintuitive that advertising would become more honest today. Nevertheless, we believe that this is exactly where we should be heading toward: customers today want to experience a closeness to the product, they want honest and authentic contact points. These must be conveyed to them by marketing and visibility.

Skepticism about the honesty of advertising is justified. Remember our example in the introduction of the detergent that can wash "whiter than white"? This sentence is not just wrong on a physical level. White has been defined very precisely: physically as the highest possible sum of all wavelengths of colors in the visible part of the light, or, for graphic artists: as the hexadecimal code #FFFFFF (the maximum of all color saturation, a mixture of cyan, magenta and yellow). Hence, white has a precise and absolute definition.

Consequently, from a purely technical point of view: whiter than white is impossible.

Yet, advertising claims the exact opposite – which is why customers have a feeling that advertising may be exaggerating, misleading or embellishing at more than one point or another. When looking at ads, customers simultaneously price this exaggeration into their perception of it.

Users of the deodorant "Axe"[26] presumably know very well that they will not win over an exorbitant number of hearts by using it, even though advertising suggests just that; and if you are a hobby craftsman shopping at B&Q, you will not be able to "Just flip it,"[27] it, even though, maybe, the store will help you with "Change. Made easier."

This is precisely the problem with advertising. Like any other content and information, it is caught in an ever-increasing push for visibility by many senders. The traditional possibilities of simply generating market opportunities through visibility are becoming increasingly hopeless. While the method of making a louder and more forceful impression on potential consumers, by emphasizing and exaggerating, by being louder and more colorful, is also losing its impact.

Customers want orientation, not screaming ads

Nowadays, consumers do not want ever louder or even more adverts. As with information and content, which is also available free of charge and both anywhere and everywhere, consumers are faced with the challenge of muddling through the offers. And last but not least, content, information and advertising mix.

Today's customers are sensitized to be skeptical on many levels. They know that an advertising promise is patient.

And that it has been for very long.

Imagine a yellow mid-range car in an advert from the 1970s, a car driving over the tracks of a vehicle test facility. The speaker explains offstage:

"Ascona – Results of tough tests on the test field: problem-free hold in bends with only low steering effort. Excellent road grip with comfortable chassis design. Excellent stability, even on extreme bumps. A successful completion of years-long developmental work. [...] Both the great know-how of Opel engineers as well as exemplary equipment of testing and construction helped achieve an ambitious goal: a driving culture!"[28]

Such a commercial tried solving several challenges at once; and as this has always been and still is the case today, it is worth taking this longer look back in time: first, it suggests to the viewer that the advertised vehicle is an excellent product. The important features are quickly and clearly emphasized. After all, the advertisers have only little time to send their message in such a commercial, consequently, the time given needs to be optimally used, leading to an extensive use of broad hints.

In all due haste, the so-called "anticipated objection" is also included. The vehicle allegedly shows "excellent road grip." Viewers who have at least a little technical understanding know that this usually goes hand in hand with a sporty and uncomfortable chassis. This leads to a pre-emptive, explicit explanation in the same sentence: the safe driving behavior comes with a simultaneous "comfortable chassis design."

Claiming that the vehicle manages the balancing act between these extremes, it is up to all challenges and meets every single need. Further on, even more, maybe even as many arguments as possible, are put forward in short sentences or even single words. The readers of the text might even get the feeling that the speaker is almost rushing to name one technical feature after another so as not to lose any potential customer's attention.

To further reinforce the effect, the company wants to use its own brand for a sort of competence transfer. According to the advert, "Opel engineers" have developed this vehicle with great knowledge and were able to draw on a testing and design department that is "exemplary."

The company has created an engineering-driven product from the power of its own abilities. Suggesting that the product has turned out accordingly. In the 1970s, this probably worked really well: then, Opel's reputation was even better suited than it is now to justify such spillover of the brand onto the perceived product quality.

These are only examples of advertising contents that exhibit the transfer benefits that advertising must yield at the overlap of the company's visibility and the customer. It needs to reveal to the customers which of the company's abilities are put into which products, and, accordingly, which customer needs will be optimally satisfied – some 50 years later, that problem has not changed.

After all, the communication of this message creates a market opportunity. It must also, whenever possible, deal with and dispel the customer's skepticism, while proving the company's legitimacy to be able to solve the customer's problems at the same time. Yet, this lets advertising fall between several stools: on the one hand, the product's technical properties, having been manufactured with precise engineering, must be brought closer to an emotionally responsive customer. On the other hand, these properties have to be conveyed in competition for attention since many are vying for it with similar offers. Now, unfortunately, the simple presentation of the distinguishing data and facts may no longer be sufficient.

Therefore, even in the 1970s, one could not assume that a mere broadcasting of an advertisement would already achieve all of this for sure and, for instance, automatically lead to a product purchase as pricey as that of a car.

Yet, it seems as if advertisers have hardly changed these mechanisms since. Television advertising, like the discussed 1975 Opel commercial, faces the same challenges – only it could solve them much better nowadays.

Both then and now, what is the one thing customers do when an advert makes them become aware of a brand, when they consider buying a new vehicle, for example? They may become suspicious and let themselves be both distracted and then seduced by another brand. This customer may come across the commercial of another car company in the same advertising window of his evening program. Volkswagen or

Mercedes may be advertising a competing product in the same range and will certainly point out its excellency.

This circumstance alone could deprive the customer of their previous leanings. Now, two or even more providers claim they have something excellent to solve the customer's problem.

Already, the market opportunity is no longer as simple as we thought. The customer has a need for transport, the manufacturer has a product that seems to be able to transport five people both comfortably and casually.

For this, customers do not even have to distrust one or the other company or their products. After the two adverts, they are simply unable to decide between these seemingly optimal solutions. However, it is highly unlikely that both products are equally good, and, after all that, the customer may now be skeptical toward both.

Customers tend to look behind the product itself

So customers look for other sources, move away from the purely promotional content provided by product manufacturers and search for information. This is a very important point in the process from products to market opportunities: customers are basically looking for honesty. As a rule, customers collect arguments proving that a certain product can offer them the optimal solution to their problem, and, to this end, they look for other sources and contact points. Plus, they have to rule out certain options since they want to avoid making a mistake with their purchase but want to see their needs served in the best way possible.

Customers have become more and more competent, at least now they have more sources, possible comparisons and information about products at their disposal should they want to. It is a welcome remedy against the flood of information and advertising, and is much easier to ensure today. In the 1970s, providing as many facts as possible in a commercial to convince people to buy a product was probably the best way to go for manufacturers. Today, it feels as if they have already left this path, instead, turning to the creation of visually powerful, emotional worlds.

However, editorial articles and tests in magazines filled this gap early on. They offer more or less objective assessments of products, compare them in quite a few categories that a run-of-the-mill consumer would most probably not be able to ascertain. Suddenly, one vehicle in a car test beats the others. This is more objective and honest, and the customer knows that information which manufactures do not want to have see the light of day is being conveyed here. After all, no manufacturer will advertise that it runs the second-best engineering center or builds the fourth-best mid-range car. Independent tests do just that.

Alternatively, on the look out for an orientation, the TV viewer could ask their neighbor, who perhaps happens to be an Opel driver. In doing so, the questioner will acknowledge that the neighbor is probably not as objective as a car magazine. On the other hand, the potential car buyer may have a trusting relationship with their neighbor. They trust their judgement, have maybe received good advice from them previously and are happy to fall back on this source of information again – even though it is much more subjective, it has a different quality of trust.

One aspect, however, unites the automobile magazine and the neighbor: they are both honest, well, at least we do hope so. The former's reputation is to a large extent based on its objectivity and impartiality – unlike advertising. While the latter is trustworthy because of their personal relationship with the potential car buyer, and because there are indicators for his credibility in the past. Moreover, both sources have tested the vehicle and gained experience with it. Customers look for such honesty.

The nature and extent of customers' information needs are subject to multiple interactions: for expensive products, more comparisons are certainly made than for impulse purchases. For instance, presumably, more when it comes to the best cradle for one's offspring than for a new adult kitchen stool. There are also bizarrely complex correlations, as, for instance, with products sold as medicine which are highly tested and supposedly safe, but still people do not really want to read about side effects that have occurred during the tests and have to be listed in the packaging.

Generally, customers still want to know more and more; they are increasingly better informed, also because high-quality information is so easily to come by. They want to be able to compare and assess (dis)advantages, are always subject to the dictate of avoiding mistakes and achieving the best bargain for themselves. However, they just as much appreciate shortcuts to such an overview and perceived security.

Honesty is the key to special market opportunities, even for small companies that would never be able to afford expensive TV spots – and yet sell better in relation to their input than big competitors.

In considering this, it becomes clear that advertising today has become more honest – *because* it must react appropriately to precisely this fact in order to be taken seriously by customers, to then make sales.

Nowadays, advertising has to function differently than in the past, which is enabled by new channels of information transfer – while being reinforced more coincidentally just like that. Advertising can still be successful when it lives up to the claim of offering contact points for customers for an honest depiction of the product's real promise. And it is possible, especially for small companies and suppliers, to prevail against the assault of information and advertising, to then gain high-quality visibility. This is an important step toward successfully seizing the opportunity to use visibility for yourself – now done more easily than ever, even in the face of today's adversity.

> Over the years, customers have matured into critical consumers. There is good news: advertising works if it is seen as an honest and authentic flagship for a company's products.

Have companies learned nothing at all?

It has been insinuated: it might be concluded that companies have learned little since the 1970s. A look at today's advertising landscape reveals little change in many places – if we were to criticize that an old-style TV commercial, which just as much today as in the past lines up argument after argument to make a product interesting to potential buyers, is far too one-dimensional.

In large parts, both print and radio/television advertising seems to function today just as it did back then. Beautiful people in beautiful places, successful, desirable and above all worthy of imitation, seem to connect crucial parameters of their stereotypically successful existence to an everyday product. You just need to use this hairspray or wear that watch – then you will be just as successful. However, this form of flat, one-dimensional visibility has become obsolete.

Nevertheless, loud, colorful and somewhat exhausting advertising does still exist: pretty much every German knows the CEO's voice of the company Seitenbacher[29], Willi Pfannenschwarz – quite notoriously so. Both him and the company have become famous for his "Seitenbacher, Seitenbacher, yummy, yummy, yummy!" in a broad Swabian dialect, a rather unusual and seemingly amateur radio commercial recorded in the company's cellar. Everyone hates it, but no one ever forgets it. Both the dialect and the unusual intonation of the advertising promises seem just as out of place today as the TV family that advertises a product in a clichéd American good-humored but annoying way. Advertising is a bit like an accident: loud, disturbing – thus unforgettable.

Yet, why are companies still doing this if the criticism from the previous chapters is true?

In its radio adverts, Seitenbacher is not flashy for its own sake. Rather, this appearance plays into the company's hands, so to speak, as both the company and the advert are special in their own way, and thus honest.

Testimonials are perceived as honest and authentic

"In all earnest, how satisfied are you with your new car? I'm thinking about buying this one as well."

The neighbor from the previous example is also an interesting approach to advertising that is perceived as more honest. Fundamentally, advertising has the problem that customers would like to buy the best product, maybe the one with the best price-performance ratio – either way, preferably the best!

What would be more obvious than for advertising to claim that they have nothing less to offer than the best product?

However, there is a catch! With interpersonal relationships, someone often appears less likable when they are just a bit too blatant about themselves and their qualities, which often costs them credibility precisely because of this obvious self-praise. Since, ultimately, advertising is communication, the same laws also apply here: advertising does not always do well to talk ever louder and more self-indulgently about its own product quality. Preferably, adverts tell customers that it offers the best product – but somehow has to be more clever about it than prior.

Testimonials are one approach to resolving this conflict of objectives – conveying that one offers the best product without explicitly saying so. The German eye-wear company Fielmann has become famous, certainly also thanks to their clear advertisement and its use of a recurring concept over many years.

It shows people in front of the camera, filmed on the street, as if they had just been approached by a team of reporters. With short, seemingly spontaneous statements, they proclaim that they have good reasons for having bought Fielmann glasses or for having just visited one of its branches.

Dr. Best,[30] a both eponymous and fictitious dentist, has also become well known in German-speaking countries. In the advertisements, he, being in his practice, usually gives an apparently spontaneous lecture on the advantages of the brand's toothbrushes.[31] This part is sometimes also taken on by the equally fictitious dentist's wife.[32]

Both examples stand for the so-called "real life testimonials." Whenever possible, they depict an authentic situation and have similarities regarding their target groups, in terms of biographical and visual characteristics as well as their interests. In so doing, they appear as supposedly neutral authorities, separate from the advertiser, and, just like any good neighbor, talk about the product's advantages. They give viewers an opportunity for identification, even generating sympathy. It also helps when the "reviewer" has characteristics marking them as an expert, as in the case of a dentist in combination with toothbrushes. This in no way affects the claim of neutrality.[33]

As informed consumers, we may wonder why no one seems to see through this, yet studies have shown that testimonials do play a role. A meta-study was even able to prove that advertising (recording and evaluating mainly online and TV adverts from various smaller studies) with real-life testimonials is, on average, 10 to 25 percent more worth in terms of brand perception and recollection as well as the assessment of advertising material. The trend discovered by this study was reinforced by a later one, in which referral marketing was found to be a good bet for companies.

Half of the respondents stated that they themselves had recommended a product to someone in the course of the last year. The fact that referral leads to more sales is particularly striking with products of emotional value. These are high-quality technology products of up-to-date brands as well as cars, holiday themes or one's choice in life insurance.[34] After all, one in two respondents said that they would pay a higher product price if they got a positive recommendation from a friend for said product.

Incidentally, celebrity testimonials score even better in terms of advert credibility and resulting sales. According to the cited meta-study, they are still clearly ahead of real-life testimonials – though both are still worth more than adverts without recommendations.

People do not have unlimited time for skepticism

Why can testimonials persuade customers more than advertising, which may try to do so with arguments or emotions, without having celebrities or confidence-inspiring faces from their own peer group deliver them? When celebrities appear in advertising and describe product benefits, it seems relatively clear that they have been paid and can therefore hardly be unbiased – the opposite of credibility. However, these celebrities usually stand for certain values – youth, dynamism, eroticism or analytical thinking, sympathy or generally for something positive. Thus, the products they advertise are then automatically located somewhat in this cosmos of certain values.

When Chiara Ferragni promotes body care products or fashion accessories, these are automatically given an upgrade. As the "world's most successful influencer," according to a *Forbes* survey, her fans and followers attribute competence and expertise to her, her recommendation has value – from her knowledge, experience, successes and function as this industry's leading figure.[35] Therefore, she is perceived as honest and authentic, although it is probably clear to her followers that she is being paid.

Ultimately, this is connected to customer convenience. Of course, followers could analyze beauty products from all accessible sources, they could read through tests and compare contents – or they could just rely on the recommendation of someone as successful in the world of beauty as Chiara Ferragni.

The easiest form of visibility: a combination of orientation and entertainment

Chiara Ferragni offers her clients two valuable aspects of good visibility, leading to sales: entertainment and orientation. The former is particularly attractive to people; we want distraction and want to see the most interesting content possible. At the same time, this also competes with our need for information, fed by the necessity for decisions – especially our demand for well-founded and sound decisions. The need for information and the need for entertainment compete for our time and attention. Consumers do not have too much time during the day and are forced to choose between information and entertainment to fill it.

Consequently, it is only logical that product visibility that serves both needs at the same time hits particularly close to home of consumers. If influencers or testimonials manage to entertain their viewers and at the same time give them valuable orientation in the product cosmos, viewers are happy to accept this offer of convenient orientation. This just necessitates a certain authority from the person providing orientation; they must be a role model or expert.

At the very least, this someone should be able to connect with others in order to give out tips. This does not necessarily mean that they have to correspond to excessive beauty standards, for instance, but possibly that they should be able to assume an authentic representative function, like having gone through the same challenges. This can mean a selection of certain products for one's own hobby, health and beauty, for professional issues or anything else. The connection should be experience-based, possibly with similar challenges or a credible expertise. For instance, an orthopedist giving a well-founded expert opinion on a damaged knee may walk with a stoop himself. They just need to be able to provide guidance on causes and, above all, treatment options. There are several sources for connection or authority.

A doctor's appointment does not necessarily have to be entertaining, rather, it is founded on the authority and expertise of the person treating the patient, other formats might be able to reconcile both. These concomitantly have an answer to a potential customer's inquiry for honest information – one that comes separate from the mere presentation of potentially questionable arguments and corporate claims. This orientation can clearly be embedded in entertainment as well.

Fan4Van's success story

Fan4Van, a YouTube channel, is a good example of a clever mixture of orientation and entertainment. The convinced camper posts videos on his channel, depicting how to optimally handle a campervan and giving information on technical details as well as the technology that goes with it. In this, he is very authentic, simply because he is an avid user of this sort of travel and vehicle.

His 94,000 subscribers do not watch commercials for the individual products, which still mostly get the spotlight of his reports. Instead, they watch entertaining but much longer clips than would be possible in a regular commercial.

The video producer puts entertaining little reports online that can be as long as 20 minutes. The viewers are well entertained by the videos and they obviously like to trust his expertise as a camper – someone who follows a particularly zeitgeisty camping style and also uses his campervan as his workplace. This helps his standing because someone who works out of his campervan spends more time in it than someone else would who takes it to the North Sea for a fortnight every year – at least, we might assume that. And for many people, this desirable lifestyle is also a good contact point.

Furthermore, just the mere number of videos emphasizes the impression of an intensive and well-founded engagement with all topics regarding camping.

First and foremost, his way of presenting the topics on his YouTube channel is entertaining to his fans. For Fan4Van, however, the channel is also a business model since he adds commissioned links to the products from the video in the video descriptions.

These product references ("You can buy product X here ...") are so-called "affiliate links." Ideally, manufacturers can track the source for customers if they, after having watched an entertaining ten-minute video, now convinced that this product could also improve their own campervan, click on the given links, in turn, leading them to the manufacturer's online shop, Amazon or other sales platforms.

From a technical perspective, this is easily done and the person running the channel Fan4Van is later rewarded with a commission for the successful sales due to their recommendation.

This is just as beneficial for product manufacturers, and it cannot be ruled out that they will actively approach the people behind certain channels.

Such affiliate testimonials are generally a common way to create high-quality visibility for products. The deal between affiliates who generate visibility for products and the manufacturers is exciting for both parties: the former do not have to make a product, do not have to guarantee distribution and can still advertise something, which they are then paid for selling. The latter do not have to pay for expensive advertising, especially since there can be many affiliates working independently, simultaneously testing dozens of types of advertising on potential target groups. Not even the best advertising department in a large company would ever be able to do it this way – possibly even ending up circling back to rather weak commercials on TV.

Additionally, the aspect of honest advertising cannot be forgotten. The affiliates who, like Fan4Van, create target group-oriented posts, cleverly mixing orientation and entertainment, can take a nuanced look (e.g. on their YouTube channel) at which content works well with their viewers, what aspect makes their numbers grow and makes viewers intact particularly well. YouTube is very good at measuring precisely this sort of interaction, turning them into actual numbers, not least because it is in the platform's own interest.

Such content then lends itself particularly well as a means for advertising messages, turning product placements into good customer service, based on honest information.

The term behind this is "content marketing." First, customers are offered free content, a special form of visibility. This increases trust in the company or person running the channel, for instance. There, customers experience the company as a potential partner who seems to be willing to give something for the customer's benefit. This creates a psychological "debt" – usually, customers subconsciously do not like free goods for which they cannot return the favor. Which would, in actuality, be a later purchase. This is called reciprocity, known to customers from the free cheese samples at the cheese counter tempting them to buy.

Nowadays, these people behind channels with engaged followers and interesting content, are commonly known as influencers.

In many areas, big channels with millions of followers are no longer the most interesting way for companies to reach their potential target groups. On the one hand, such large channels are also concerned with their own authenticity, thus, increasingly avoiding adverts for one brand on day X and for a competing brand on day Y. Followers tend to notice such quick changes and, subsequently, (re)evaluate the successful influencer's credibility quite rigorously.

However, for successful influencers, this quickly exhausts potential customers of effective product adverts. In addition, people running highly professional channels, sometimes having entire social media teams behind them, have not always been able to retain the charm of small, self-made content. Influencers and their channels always trade some authenticity for a perfect and well-lit presentation.

The three dimensions of valuable visibility

The previous chapter has shown that the concept of smart visibility is replacing loud, low-value visibility.

Smart visibility is any visibility that customers, on the one hand, like to see and so is not perceived as annoying but rather as an interesting gain, and that, on the other hand, leads them to buy.

Visibility needs three dimensions for this to work, and only in the combination of these is worthless visibility turned into high-quality, smart visibility:

- Relevance. Only topics that are interesting to your customers will ultimately lead to purchases. A parrot owner, for instance, may be annoyed by repeatedly seeing dog training content because it is irrelevant to their interests. Instead, something that shows them how to train their parrot to speak could be of great relevance to them. A migraine patient has no interest in information on how to deal with tinnitus or rheumatism: both do not pertain to their pain history. However, they are very interested in soothing their migraine due to its impact on their lives. Digital channels of visibility such as TikTok or Instagram have made it one of their highest priorities for their algorithms to present users with individually relevant content.
- Authority. If the relevance criterion applies (then and only then – the other criteria do not work without relevance), people listen to role models above all else: to authorities. So, for instance, the migraine patient will trust a neurologist who specializes in said migraines. Or they listen very carefully to a person who is themselves a migraine

patient and has managed to take control of the disease. In both cases, this adds the sender's authority to relevance.

- Storytelling. People highly value stories and entertainment – large markets such as those for novels or Hollywood films function exclusively on the basis of a (mostly fictional) story. This, in combination with the first two criteria, is like an amplifier for smart visibility.

The combination of these three dimensions in an as large an overlap as possible creates smart visibility, which, as a direct consequence, is followed by a product purchase.

Visibility needs relevance

Who would ever watch 447,000 videos on any topic, for instance, in order to understand investment opportunities? And who would ever look at 227 million websites to find out how to become an author? Admittedly, every single video creator and every single runner of a web-

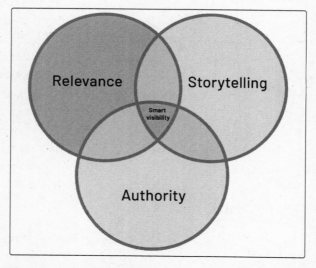

The first criterion for smart visibility is relevance – authority and storytelling add to it. Smart visibility happens when all three overlap.

Source: original illustration

site, blog or just Facebook account that can be found with a search engine achieves visibility for their topic on Google – at least theoretically. If you are not among the first few hits in the Google search results list, you will most likely never be found.

As has already been hinted at, the plethora of information and the democratic chance of making one's information visible leads to another problem: access rates for web pages, for instance, that appear on the second page of Google's search results list are statistically already below 1 percent of total clicks of the overall search results. And this statistics obviously does not improve for Google's possibly hundreds of other search result pages – and we are only talking about one average search entry. Once again, the Internet with its (theoretically possible) visibility has its downside: all those not right at the top of the list are invisible.

Establishing relevance is the second step taken by Google and other search engines when dealing with information, i.e. ranking content for visibility. Highly developed algorithms, which increasingly strive for artificial intelligence, filter and sort information to then present it tailored to each individual Google user. First off, this is a truly impressive service. Google takes its users' personal and demographic characteristics into account, scans and analyzes the websites' information, and then tries to match said information with search queries.

Being a free-of-charge search engine is obviously not a suitable business model for Google. However, this is exactly where Google can create relevance for its customers, establishing another, relevant business model. If a user experiences Google as a preferred channel for quick and unerring information gathering on certain topics, then they will associate Google with relevance – for their problem of the first order, namely the search query just made. And also for their problem of the second order, namely finding and filtering the insane amount of information found online.

Google offers its customers a direct shortcut to information, thus satisfying customer needs, and strives to suggest the most relevant hit out of 447,000 video results for each user. Just how impressively precise Google's approach is can be seen each time we pull astonished faces when Google has already anticipated the topics we are talking about:

"One minute we're talking about our holiday, and the next Google gives me hotel suggestions ..."

Just as impressive and illuminating in terms of this service's precision is the fact that Facebook, which is also highly developed in its use of similar algorithms, can probably predict its users' behavior better than their closest (real, not virtual) friends. For instance, after only ten likes, Facebook can predict a user's behavior better than a work colleague would. After about 150 likes – and that can be an afternoon of using Facebook for some users – it is better at the predictions than someone's siblings. And after 300 interactions with the platform, Facebook can make a better personality analysis than the user's own life partner.[1]

While researchers at Cambridge University took the circuitous route in researching this and were only able to tap into certain Facebook data with a meta-software, Facebook's algorithms can draw on user data much better and with less obstructions. This goes to show the amount of power that modern networks like Google and Facebook have – just from the data they collect and the algorithms they continually develop with it.

So what about the business model? Google and Facebook can be extremely precise in their filtering of information for users – and then sell this now predictable user behavior and interests to advertisers. This is how Google achieves relevance: users alone cannot provide orientation in the noise of all that accessible information. So they experience Google itself as a relevant provider for their need for orientation in the jungle of the plethora of information.

The good news for companies: they could also do this! And without having to trade in information for it.

Not visibility but relevance is the key

Largely due to the Internet and now more than ever, consumers are faced with having to filter products, services and information. And ultimately, their only valid option for achieving this is picking and choosing information channels. Consumers know that by choosing one information channel, they are actively excluding several others. This is quite human; all users have their own value patterns, biases, sources, friends as well as even popular and tenaciously adhered to misconceptions. However, the search of relevance in conjunction with visibility means that it is now every company's goal to obtain this form of privileged visibility. Ideally, customers should be able to assume that, in regards to a certain topic, they are always in good hands with a certain company – a phenomenon called branding.

When looking for a particularly high-end garment, customers will think of brands that may also project this message. "I'm looking for an exquisite piece of clothing, maybe something from Louis Vuitton!" Ultimately, the company Louis Vuitton could care less about the customer's reasons for buying their clothes, whether it is the cut, their faith in the quality or because they want to impress the people around them. The most important aspect is that customers have to assume that Louis Vuitton will do the best job for them, i.e. stay relevant to them.

For particularly healthy food, a customer thinks of their town's organic food shop, where they have had positive experiences, thus, this shop gives them orientation; this might go so far that they buy products unchecked. The experiences with the supplier were positive, which established a connection as the shop became relevant to the customer when they were looking for particularly healthy, sustainable or carefully produced products. Now, this shop serves as a filter of the mass of products for the customer, for instance, because the shop only sells organic produce. This way, customers do not have to do the otherwise necessary research, the organic shop provides orientation and safety against mistakes regarding this need.

This is a practical hallmark of relevance. Almost every company and almost every service provider can generate visibility and be seen by potential customers when they use this guidance function and resulting relevance. Plus, the latter clearly transforms visibility from worthless to valuable. Businesses do this by trying to put together a relevant selection for their customers, and Google does this by ranking relevant information for its users.

Valuable visibility from relevance

From the early 2000s, Google pioneered the idea of showing specific adverts to people with potential interests – and tracking these interests beforehand. Google calls this targeting, which made *the* difference – and drove traditional media into today's economic crisis. The simple reason behind it being that when customers see Google as relevant regarding the filtering of information and in their orientation for certain questions, they will also trust the shown content the same, even though Google lets advertisers pay for it.

Now, this is a business model – and one of the most successful ones worldwide at that.

For companies that had previously booked adverts in American magazines, for instance, the added value of placing their advertising here became immediately obvious: they were increasingly cornered by the growing need for visibility for evermore products and services, alongside all the other increasingly visible information and contents.

On the one hand, it is hardly useful to show an advert for a product on television to millions of people because this also means a huge scattering loss. After all – albeit, not only with television but also with radio, newspapers, etc. – the price is not calculated from the number of interested parties but from the total number of potential addressees. This is the so-called "cost per mille" (CPM; cost per thousand people reached, sometimes also referred to as "cost per thousand").

Roughly speaking, this used to be the price of an advertising minute in television, scaled according to broadcasting time and average interest of viewers in certain programs, measured by audience ratings. Television was able to quantify and thus commercialize this. This meant that adverts during one of the big Saturday night shows was more expensive than at other times.

It did not matter whether the advert was about a niche product or about one that all viewers would love to snatch up. The CPM remained the same.

Yet, this truly becomes a problem when you want to sell cat food during a program that six million dog owners but no cat owners are watching. The advertising price for a television slot remains unaffected by this, but here nothing gets sold. This is the so-called reach marketing, in which just the reach as such and, consequently, unguided, untargeted visibility are paid for.

In contrast, Google, just like Facebook later on, was much better at avoiding marketing with a scattering effect, and instead shows relevant advertising content to the customers the companies wanted to address. After all, who if not Google and Facebook knew whether cat or dog owners were sitting there, looking at the screen. They just typed in a search query or scrolled through their newsfeed, briefly stuck to certain relevant posts or even interacted with them, liked, commented or shared. And on Google, they clicked on links, scrolled through pages and opened or closed others.

Easy to imagine in regards to Google: when a user types in a search query, precisely *this* topic is relevant to them at *this* moment in time. When they ask Google for "Best cat food," then an advert for high-quality cat food is probably also highly relevant to them. As a frequent user, they assume that Google will provide them with relevant content anyway, leading to a great degree of loyalty. Customers appreciate Google's guidance function, which also enables Google to get a certain amount of trust from the advertising company in the users. Both factors are a service for which advertising companies now spend a lot of money, since the relevance criterion is met.

Facebook's targeting does not refer to specific search queries – even Google has not used it as its only source for a long time – instead, it simply observes its users and collects large quantities of statistical data about them. Customers have preferences, give biographical details and make interests transparent to the company through their behavior on the platform and other movements online. For quite a while now, the Internet has not only been producing huge amounts of data but has also been collecting and commercializing it as "Big Data."

Both companies show cat food ads to cat owners. Here, the idea of a directly emerging market opportunity between a company's abilities and customer needs suddenly fits much better: Google and Facebook match both profiles much more precisely than it could ever happen by chance with unguided visibility.

The two exemplary platforms obviously have a particularly good hold on the sales process. Simultaneously, Facebook connects people with each other and with its own offers. People, using their phone to look at their friends' lives and that of other people around the world, feel a connection to them *and* to the app. Last but not least, Facebook is considered a social network, bringing social interaction into the digital – thus, meeting the users' basic need for social interaction.

Google's greatest strength lies in its relevance, as it provides its users with tons of information to each search query and also gives orientation in this jungle of information. The decline of the telephone book alone shows that relevant information which can be passed on quickly and securely is easily accepted. Nowadays, no one would check the telephone book listings for restaurants – be it because no one owns one anymore or because Google can tell us all about the restaurant, like opening times, reviews and directions, thus, far more than the book ever could. Instead, it bundles much less interesting information. At best, it gives the address, but apart from that it can neither give directions nor suggest what else would be interesting to know.

Ultimately, due to this effect, Google, like Facebook, has authority over its users, meeting the criterion of authority in passing: as soon as two people get into a discussion about something, the phone is quickly pulled out of the pocket for a search for reputable sources. At this point, it is no secret that this scenario plays out differently each time. In any case, Google will quickly provide good contact points for its users. By doing this, Google, like Facebook and many comparable networks, creates an excellent environment for the placing of advertising content.

Highly relevant ads have devastating effects on reach marketing

Relevant marketing beats reach marketing every time – being an important proof for the criterion of relevance for visibility.

This illustration shows the market for advertising in daily newspapers in the US since 1950, denoted by the dark line moving unsteadily upwards from 1950 to around the turn of the millennium – from a solidly increasing average between 20 and its final peak of 67 billion dollars. Smaller annual fluctuations hardly matter and even the odd good upward peak can be detected. Bottom line, the market for news-

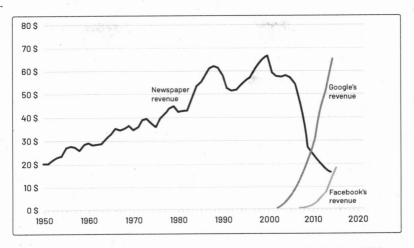

Development of advertising sales in traditional newspapers in the US since 1950, inflation-adjusted for 2014, in billions of US dollars.

Source: original illustration according to an idea and illustration on the blog Carpe Diem, based on the data by the Newspaper Association of America as well as the publicized revenues of Google and Facebook[2]

paper advertising has been growing solidly for decades: golden times for newspaper publishers.

However, around the year 2000, this changes abruptly with Google entering the advertising stage. The appearance of this new medium clearly threatens traditional advertising. Google's turnover, i.e. its ability to turn companies and their advertising into its own profit, increases drastically as soon as Google recognizes this opportunity for itself. Apparently, it has found an improvement on how previous media did advertising. It is no longer a secret: obviously, they have a better grip on relevance toward potential customers than daily newspapers.

This analysis is conclusive after the previously described correlations. There was no way that Google would not have become successful, given all its parameters of good visibility and their potential implementation. Google can use relevance marketing without having to rely on reach.

Google does not have to scatter ads to as many users as possible, which they might find either irrelevant or even annoying. Instead, Google constantly strives for the one ideal: showing the right advert for the right product to the right customer at the right time – thus, making the concluding purchase based on the highest possible relevance almost inevitable.

Ultimately, its rapid rise to the top of all advertising platforms was the logical step because Google is just too successful with it, and because companies who advertised with them immediately understood this, which is reflected in Google's increasing number of customers.

Facebook followed a similar path with a slightly different method,

Locations
Location
• United States

Age
18–65+

Gender
All genders

Detailed Targeting
Include people who match

Demographic data > Education > Education level

University degree

Interests > Additional interests

Bonsai

Orchids

Q Add demographics, interests or behaviors   Suggestions   Browse

Professional qualification	☐
Doctoral degree	☐
University degree	☑
In postgraduate studies	☐

Online adverts can be shown very precisely to specific target groups, thus avoiding any scattering effect. In this example, an Instagram ad is only shown to people in Germany with a university degree who are interested in bonsai and orchids, and who are aged 18 and over.

Source: Facebook Business Manager

which is also depicted in the illustration above. Here, advertising has also always been placed and displayed with a focus on maximum relevance and accuracy for potential customers. And here, big data was also used on a large scale for the creation of a database.

Two aspects are insightful when it comes to creating visibility for one's own company or person in a similarly successful manner as Google and Facebook – though perhaps not with similar sales figures but regarding their methodology. First, digitization alone is not the key to success. Magazines in the US, too, have naturally been using digital channels. This is depicted in the illustration above as well since 2000, but it decreases nearly parallel with the analog advertising budgets. To put it plainly: newspapers could not be saved by just digitizing what they had always been doing.

This is interesting because digitization is seen by many companies as both an opportunity and a threat. Entrepreneurs and companies have been sensitized to the fact that it is a necessary step to go digital, if they want to stay relevant in the long run, that is – not least after having witnessed market developments like the one for newspapers and magazines. At the same time, people who might just be starting out with their own (small) companies are watching the same processes and are certain: digitalization is a backbone of entrepreneurial success, or at least the basis of successful marketing.

Obviously, though, the mere use of digital channels and tools is not the magic bullet against corporate threats. It is insufficient to simply replace processes that worked well previously but now face competition. It is much more a matter of using digital processes *together with* functioning analog processes, thus transporting and complementing their strengths in new ways. Digitization is only powerful where it complements and strengthens a company's or service's already developed advantages, instead of just replacing them.

That is the real position of power occupied by Facebook and Google with their algorithms and tools. They convey and show quicker, more unerringly and more reliably what people have always been looking for: relevant content.

Newspapers became a leading medium for generations because they brought information and sometimes entertainment safely and, for their time, quickly to their readers. However, today, other channels can do it quicker: YouTube, news apps and news tickers bring information even faster. "... I don't need to read the newspaper, I can get info that much faster through the *Sky News* app" is just one of the many sentences that show the harsh reality for daily newspapers today. A fulfillment of the promise of relevance used to be more random: subscribers of a magazine like *The Economist*, for instance, showed a certain affinity for economic topics. This has become more difficult even for daily newspapers, and the promise of relevance disappears in the fog of general information. This is already recognizable from the different newspaper sections such as "local," "politics," "sports" and "feature" as well as its classic use at the breakfast table: "Can I have the local section while you read the sports section?"

Simply offering a digital version of the daily newspaper, through a website for instance, does not safe the system from its downfall as one would hope. It is true that in terms of speed and ubiquitous accessibility of information, this brings the newspaper up to speed with channels like YouTube, Google, Facebook and Instagram. Yet, the information is still bound to a "print logic": in a sense, it is waiting for a reader to find their way to it of their own accord, like checking out the website.

Google and Facebook, on the other hand, offer their customers the interesting information without them having to actively look for it. In its feed, Facebook shows information and sponsored advertising posts side by side and specifically for those likely to have a use for it, or Google ads are integrated on a website, which are selected for each visitor just as specifically. And ideally, users do not even perceive them as annoying because they are based on a very precise analysis, the recommendation of Big Data and the two advertising giants' algorithms.

That is still not all: digital channels can also use the temporal component as a success factor. If the *Sky News* app can be opened whenever users have time, if it is both small and compact and carries an infinite amount of information in one's pocket, if it offers an infinite number of possible connections for further research by embedding the Internet, and if it perhaps also provides users with news that corresponds to their interests, then this turns the digital into an uphill battle for newspapers.

Last but not least, newspapers, at least in their analog form, are a product bound to raw materials and tangible carriers, which are just as financed by advertising like an app or a website. A magazine's so-called "marginal costs," those nearly irreducible minimum costs that have to be recouped through sales, are plagued heavily by those carriers.

All these factors have had a devastating effect on traditional advertising. Not only did the industry have to admit defeat in terms of costs, it also had to cut back on delivery time. There are major differences in access and process when an editor triggers a lengthy printing process and the dispatch of a physical print product with the confirmation of the latest news in an editorial office – or when the content can immediately be found online. Yet, above all – especially in regards to the influence on the whole process – stands relevance; Facebook and Google made sure of that with their users.

Relevance is the fundament of smart visibility

So what are the basic mechanisms which have shaped Google's and Facebook's great success and which, to a good extend, can be copied from them? First and foremost, relevance: it must be a top priority to offer the right product to the right customer at the right time. This is a prerequisite for smart, high-quality visibility.

There is good news: if this has been achieved, if relevance has been generated as precisely as possible for clearly identified target groups, then, at least in general, only a few customers need to be addressed for a good business success.

It s better to close eight sales for every ten prospects you approach than to get the same result after approaching 10,000 prospects. Relevance can make *that* difference. Incidentally, this is also reflected in the cost structure: advertising is compensated across channels according to the CPM – if it is sufficient to reach a few contacts, then that, in turn, makes it cheaper.

Which brings us to more good news: when using the new digital possibilities, the CPM can make *the* difference for small companies because only spaces for relevant advertising content need to be booked and shown to interested users. It is far cheaper to show a precisely targeted advertising campaign to 500 Facebook users than to 20,000 newspaper readers who, unfortunately, are more interested in the sports section or the obituaries.

Now, these performance-oriented channels are available to everyone. If the requirements of relevance are taken into account, successful advertising is easier and cheaper than ever.

Adverts need anchors

However, Facebook and Google do not display advertising in its pure form, even though they would probably like to do just that, as it would counteract precisely their business models. Advertisers pay for the fact that Facebook and Google have already statistically tracked customer characteristics and can allocate them to their different offers.

One could assume that it would be exciting for Facebook and Google, with this business model in mind, to constantly show such advertising. However, users would probably not tolerate it, as such an offer of information would now be much less attractive. (On a side note: Facebook users would be much less interested in solely advertising content than Google users.) Google usually lists two or three sponsored links at the top of the search results – but alongside many other organic search results (i.e. unpaid ones).

What if all search results were sponsored in this form? Would Google make even more revenue? Instead, Google opts for the preservation of its intact aura of comprehensive information and the supposed equality of information – users would probably not see only sponsored content as objective source material.

On Facebook, a lot of the content is shown from companies, institutions and groups as well as private people after users have subscribed to the content they want to see. Yet, in between, Facebook sprinkles in adverts precisely tailored to these users. If all messages from friends, interesting information channels and groups were to disappear, Facebook would jeopardize its relevance as a source of interesting information for its users – even though Facebook might find it interesting from a business perspective.

Thus, Google and Facebook have to find the right combination of both extremes, creating a balance that is perceived as such by the user.

Two things can be learned from both firms: relevant information beats broadly spread general information. And promotional content should often be presented with a disguise, cloaked in entertaining and informative content to keep customers connected and interested.

Second-order relevance increases customer interest

However, relevance cannot be limited to just content – that would be too short-sighted. Yes, it is true that content is closely linked to first-order relevance – previous sections have shown this in detail.

The second important order in relation to relevance is its temporal aspect.

Imagine yourself sitting at the dinner table with your family, and then the phone rings. Grudgingly you answer it – you do not want to interrupt your pleasant family time, but you still want to know whether it is urgent.

An insurance agent is on the line and he offers you a quite interesting new insurance for your car, which would save you several hundred euros each year. Plus, you have already been thinking of changing your car insurance, so his offer is indeed relevant.

In our example, the agent even works at the insurance company that already works for you, he is accordingly well-informed about existing contracts. This gives him credibility and sound knowledge, his offer is valuable and relevant in terms of content. Only, the timing is bad. So you ask him to call again some other time because you just sat down for your family meal.

In terms of content, the insurance agent's offer has recognizable relevance, it is just missing temporal relevance. Already, the game between pressure marketing and pull marketing shifts to the company's disadvantage. The customer actively blocks the (actually interesting) offer and the company has to make another attempt at contacting the customer at a later date: "I'll be happy to call again later!"

This is unattractive because it costs company resources and because it can turn into a disruptive aspect in the customer's life, thus, reducing the company's chances of a sale. Sometimes, the customer has to actively approach the company now: "No, leave it, I'll get back to you!"

Let us further assume there is an exciting feature film on television the same night. As it is a private channel, the film is regularly interrupted by windows of advertisements. It was probably produced in the USA, where films are routinely produced for such advertising windows. At the most exciting points, just when a plot development is reaching its climax, the commercial break is switched on – the "cliffhanger" to keep the customer on the line: a sympathetic character from the film is just hanging over a cliff and it is questionable whether they can save themselves. And … that's when the commercials start.

The idea behind it is quite obvious. The viewer is meant to stay seated in front of the television during the commercial break to see whether their favorite protagonist is going to survive. This is meant to increase the connection to the adverts as producers are otherwise unsure whether viewers would not just get up and leave to do something else during the adverts.

Yet, that is also where the problem lies. The adverts are shown at the most inopportune moments, they disrupt. And disruptive marketing is perceived as spam by consumers – even when its contents are relevant. Even if the idea of changing the car insurance provider is still in the room, now is just not the time to think about it!

The situation can be completely different just a few weeks later. The customer is sitting at the car dealership of their choice and has just bought their dream car. The dealer pledges to make it a quick transaction and says that now only the license plate, the payment and an electronic insurance confirmation are needed.

Suddenly, annoying spam marketing from the same insurance company, which, only a few weeks ago, was completely out of place when it advertised on TV, turns into an interesting offer. The same customer who had previously reacted with annoyance now wants contact with the insurance company – pressure marketing has turned into pull marketing. The insurance agent who was turned away at the dinner table is now suddenly a highly interesting partner for conversation. The offer has relevance now for the customer in terms of content and time due to a small alteration in the system – with the customer taking out the insurance.

For the concept of smart visibility, this means that relevance (both in terms of content and time) is an important island in the sea of worthless visibility. And these islands offer valuable and smart visibility. Relevance is fundamental because a customer will only consider doing business with a company when they are sure that a problem can be solved for them by said company. They will only buy when the time is right for problem solution.

Visibility is upgraded by authority

Should a person with authority enter a room, you will usually notice quite quickly: not by that person's behavior as such but by the reactions of those around them.

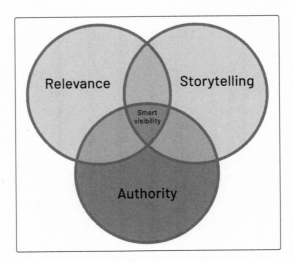

Authority pays into the dimensions of relevance and storytelling.

Source: original illustration

Imagine you are invited to a reception in England, which will also be attended by the King of England. Excited by the prospects of this invitation, you arrive early – as have many others. In a banquet hall, everyone is standing together, maybe having a welcome drink and conversing.

But wait, why is this such a striking example? Mainly because only very few people are ever invited to such a reception in the presence of the Queen. The Queen, as a person of high authority, which she derives essentially from her office, is not at all easy to find. She does not invite people to her home all the time, and when she does, then it is only a very select group of people: authorities make themselves scarce.

However, during the welcome drinks, the Queen has not yet arrived. Still, attention is already focused on her. Everyone is waiting for the first signs of her appearance. Which door might be opened for her? From where will her entourage appear? It would be a lofty goal to exchange a few words with her – probably not so much because certain topics need to be discussed in detail, but rather to be able to tell others afterwards that you exchanged a few words with the Queen. In the later narrative, this would clearly put importance on each of the guests who were important enough for the authority to have paid attention to them, and who have taken on some of her glamour in the process.

This is also a distinguishing feature of authorities: even if not present, they can draw attention to themselves, to others and to certain contexts.

This authority also influences both space and time, even conveys the event's tenor. If she is not there yet, the event has somehow not really begun. If she would not come at all, it would, in retrospect, clearly devalue the event – for everyone. It would also clearly devalue the story that could be told of this event afterwards: "I was once invited to a reception that the Queen was meant to attend, too."

Authorities give meaning to contexts that they would not have without them.

When the time has finally come for the authority to appear, this is perhaps initially revealed by bodyguards entering the room or a sudden flurry of activity. Finally, there she is, the Queen, and all attention is focused on her. She may say a few words of welcome without interruption. When present, the authority is accorded the highest respect and listened to.

However, this does not just go for the Queen. Other authorities are also distinguished by the fact that they can be quiet and still be heard. Think back to a particularly interesting guest at the last family party who everyone rallied around when they spoke quietly and thoughtfully. Their input has relevance. Something that distinguishes authority: people are looking for an opportunity to engage with and to listen to their input.

First, let us stick to observations: all this is supported by a clear framing of authority. Just like a frame often defines the picture, many external circumstances often make authorities recognizable as what they are. However, we should not picture this frame metaphor too narrowly.

For instance, the "Mona Lisa" in the Louvre also has a frame, but most people would have to google it to know what it looks like. It is not particularly spectacular, and it would certainly be presumptuous to assume that the picture has become so famous due to its frame. Yet, the picture has a larger frame in *the place* where it is hung. And, incidentally, the location is part of the frame.

If you go to the world-famous Louvre, then you probably do so not least of all because of the "Mona Lisa". Upon entering the room where this iconic painting hangs, you can see many paintings on the left side, large and spectacular paintings, hanging abundantly and lavishly side by side. While at the front of the room awaits you exactly one picture: the "Mona Lisa". It is quite differently hung, set apart from the viewers, it is protected by a bullet-proof glass pane and most eyes in the room are drawn to this (by the way, rather small) picture.

Just as in Gothic cathedrals the visitor's gaze is automatically directed upwards upon entering (essentially due to the window design – long, high and narrow), here attention is also directed by framing. This is how it works with authorities, too: they bind and direct attention.

Frames in which we encounter authorities are also supported by other features. These can be certain insignia, such as a doctor's white coat or a judge's robe.

Upon entering a bank, it does make a difference whether you talk to someone standing at the customer counter at the front or whether you are allowed to go to one of the back rooms where you are amicably welcomed by a customer advisor.

You may even get the chance to speak to the bank manager. They have more authority than their staff, they can decide more and possibly solve other problems for customers.

In this case, the framing of their office determines the perceived authority toward their customers. Framing can shape and support a person's or an institution's authority in various ways.

Authority needs time

Time is another important factor. Sometimes this becomes clear from inconspicuous details, take the previously mentioned bank manager, for instance – you will probably have assumed he is a bit older. At least when you enter the bank and risk a first glance around, checking for the possible manager with whom you are about to have an appointment, you may unconsciously look for people who do not look as if they have just started their training. Visibility, authority and attention have a very subtle effect.

The reason for your targeted search for an older employee is simply the assumption that it takes time to climb the career ladder in such an institution. After all, the bank will not allow itself to put someone unexperienced and without in-depth knowledge in such an important position. The decisive factor, which also influences authority, is time and it indirectly conveys other values such as competence, experience and vision.

Incidentally, these are mere clichés and stereotypes. Some banks cannot find enough experienced people to always put someone with 30 years in the profession in charge. Or these experienced people are needed in even higher positions in the bank – thus, a young employee becomes branch manager in a small rural branch. This does not mean that they lack competence or their advice lacks quality. Yet, it is still interesting to see how many clichés customers have in mind and the degree of authority they grant others.

So in addition to framing, time often factors in as the second pillar of strong authority. Many companies know this and design their marketing accordingly. The most visible example of which can often be found in the company logo which then highlights cues like "since 1876" or "Est. 1912."

The factor time intersects between authority and stories, which we will deal with in the next part of the book. Age, experience and past successes only bind authority through stories; and because these characteristics can be found in the past, they need a means of transport for current visibility to potential customers.

Authorities can commend themselves as objective sources if they can, to this extent, attach stories and time to themselves. People who have seen a lot and gained just as much experience like to be perceived as experts. During this long time, successes and also challenges, perhaps even mistakes and failures, could have taken place, which, in sum, support honest authority. It provides safety in terms of relevant information and honest marketing.

Yet, it can do even more because authority has the power to lead customers onto a certain field of perception where objectivity has lost its importance, since they willingly follow the authority's (even biased) guidance function. When people or companies can use authority for themselves to this extent, it gives them a certain moral responsibility, since they also gain privileged access to the possibility of defining relevance and telling credible stories.

You have to become an authority

A while ago, one of Banksy's pictures was auctioned off. The artist themselves is still unknown and keeps in the dark, yet, their art is infamously well known.

Banksy's "Girl with balloon" was handed over to be auctioned off in its frame. Here, too, the frame itself was not especially spectacular, could not increase the picture's worth – at least not right away.

After the auction was finished, the picture suddenly started to glide through the bottom part of the frame that was a well-hidden shredder. Half of the picture was then shredded into the stripes which have since hung from the frame at the bottom. Just moments before, the picture had been sold for 1.2 million euros, and after it had been partly destroyed, it did not become worthless – not by a long shot. Indeed, its worth had multiplied by factor 20.[3]

From the technical side, it might have been the frame, but the increase in value emerged from the process itself that viewers watched in horror. It was the scope of action and the framing which substantiated the artist's authority.

Stories that grow around something like a sort of frame can have a large influence on the status of an authority. When we separate authority and stories as pillars of smart visibility in our considerations and still accentuate each, then the two intersect right then and there.

The factor of time and diverse stories that occur during this time play an important role in the perception of a person's or company's authority. In these stories, an authority is clearly associated with characteristics, which then give guidance. This is also the case with authorities completely unknown to and intangible for us.

The artist Banksy is a nebulous figure. The person behind the pseudonym has not been conclusively found out – whether it is an artist collective, a female or male artist. What is clear, however, is that they have a different approach to art and bring it to the people fully independent of traditional structures and convictions. For instance, their graffiti, which appear in unusual places and refer to political or social themes, have become (in)famous. They have placed unsolicited and unauthorized art in museums, sprayed statements on walls in political crisis regions, thus, elevating a special form of street art to an iconic level of pop culture.

That is coherent and also part of authority and framing. Authorities are compelling: the fact that Banksy thinks about art differently from others, that they break with patterns and both repeatedly and spectacularly attract attention is an integral part of their art. So, buyers make a clear statement when they hang a Banksy on their living room wall. Art can have a radiating effect on customers, it can stand for a critical view of things, it can ennoble the buyer as a controversial and free spirit. Authorities stand for core values.

Yet, it is quite impossible to hang a Banksy on one's living room wall because their art is often stencil graffiti sprayed on a house wall or somewhere else outside. It is difficult to remove them from there and frame them as is tradition – in this respect, Banksy is quite rigorous and predictable.

Suddenly, however, their art was up for bid in this auction, a break with their previous style. Until the moment half of the transportable picture on paper was shredded – thus reducing it to absurdity and turning it back into a consistent and "typical" Banksy. Perhaps Banksy's art is much more conservative and less pattern-breaking than fans of their art might like?

Should that be the case, then it has above all integrity, which also constitutes the artist's authority. We feel as if we know what to expect – in this case, a surprise. For people, this still fundamental and style-forming integrity is a very pleasant feeling on many levels and a comfortable (because stereotypical) prospect. People usually appreciate the security and guidance function that lies in such a clearly delineated horizon of expectations. "I have a Banksy hanging above my sofa …" – "Ah, isn't that this totally nonconformist street artist where we never know where they're gonna show up next and what they're gonna to do there …?" For customers, authority is also derived from clarity, integrity and reliability.

Customers want beacons of authority

Customers look for such beacons. In an inflation of visible content and promotional messages as we have described prior, institutions with a guidance function are a godsend for customers. The latter can use the former to achieve shortcuts to feelings and certainties they want to associate with a product purchase or service booking.

When you buy a Banksy, you can be sure what statement comes with it. Anyone who buys a Mercedes Benz has a clear sense of what kind of product with which attributes they are getting for their money and also which message they are sending to the world. Anyone who asks a recognized heart specialist for an expert opinion on their expert topic does so in the urgent pursuit of orientation. Patients do *not* want to hear: "Don't be nervous, this is my first heart surgery as well!"

Yet, integrity is indispensable for this guidance function. When customers are looking for orientation, authorities with integrity need to give them just that. This is the only way to clearly outline the frame(work) within which the authority can then assume a guidance function for customers through experience, competence and charisma.

Authority has structure

Authority can best be observed by its ability to guide attention. On the other hand, it can best be defined by the way it determines its environment: authorities have a profound power of interpretation. They define a discourse's content, they shape contexts, thus, influencing other people's decisions in these fields. If, for instance, Karl Lagerfeld proclaimed that green was the color of this summer, then green would be the color of this summer – for his discourse and for all those who saw and recognized his authority.

This is particularly prevalent in the arts. Here, many discourses are particularly difficult to grasp and define. The all too frequent feeling of "I can do that too …" while looking at, particularly, modern art is a symptom of such uncertainties. When a painting like "Onement VI" by Barnett Newman – a blue surface divided by one light greenish-blue vertical line – is auctioned off at Sotheby's for 44 million dollars, this calls for orientation and explanation for many viewers. Both create an authority – for instance, an art expert's expertise printed in the museum guide.

Yet, what leads to such a value for one piece of art? The answer is linked to guided attention.

For instance, when a young artist has their very first exhibition, chance helps sometimes. Maybe they are able to find a renown venue to show their work. This way, they maybe get their first media attention for their art and get invited to their first art contest. There, honorable art professors, thus, authority figures, might be present as part of the jury, and one of them recognizes great art in one of the artist's works. Maybe this particular work speaks to them due to their own personal passions or their own expertise.

In any way, this motivation might enable this professor to prevail over the others' opinions or convince them to crown this work as the winner of the competition.

After that, this piece of art is sold in an auction and maybe chance helps here as well: two bidders are interested in it, and a bidding war ensues. The achieved selling price will henceforth be a point of orientation for pieces by this particular artist, thus, a going price has been established for their work.[4]

Since only few objective criteria that can be derived directly from artistic creativity play a role in this whole process, and because chance is rather an important factor, the value of such a work results mainly from the involved players' authority. The professors who took part in the competition as well as the auction bidders, the auction house with its expertise and an estimated price as well as the discussion of the painting in art magazines – all of these have an authoritative effect on the art work's value.

Artistic expression and quality are not too often written by chance, as this example may have shown. Though, chance can certainly play a role when it is reinforced by authority, for instance – because authorities have interpretive power like the art professor in the example above.

Furthermore, authority is to some extent hereditary. Some companies like to use celebrities to benefit from their authority in a particular field. Some companies use their founder as a source of authority and also interpretational sovereignty. If Michael Jordan claims that Nike's sports shoes are his first choice for basketball, then the shoes "inherit" the basketball legend's authority. When the tough jury of experienced entrepreneurs in the TV format *Dragons' Den* or *Shark Tank* for instance, grants ambitious founders an investment (thus, ennobling them), the product inherits the investors' authority – as well as the authority of their founders with all their qualities, who have enthusiastically developed a good product, now eager to present it.

Yet, inherited authority only works to some extent, and it can be useful especially at the beginning because it creates visibility. Authority has a significant advantage over the challenge of smart visibility: when someone with a lot of authority points out the relevant, they share a certain instant relevance out of thin air with it.

Therefore, authority interacts with visibility. Just as it can direct visibility (showing strategic advantages not least for marketing contexts), it in itself also essentially lives off visibility. If, as in our art example, visibility is the starting point for an initial authority because, for instance, it powerfully generates attention as an inherited authority, then, conversely, this should also mean that persons and brands need to always keep an eye on their own visibility to become authorities themselves. You can only become an authority when you are visible.

The choice of the right niche is the first important step. It is easier to become visible and an authority in a small niche than it is in a large market segment in which many competitors are fighting for visibility. It is also easier to become visible in a sharply defined niche.

Additionally, it is also important with whom and in which environment you are seen. Visibility in the *wrong* environments has the same effect on authority as in the right one because it always adds up – albeit, without any control on your part. Therefore, you need to think carefully about whether you would rather achieve large but devaluing visibility in a third-rate reality show or little visibility at a professional symposium – even though the net reach is certainly better with the former, it is by far more valuable with the latter.

So the choice of stage should be made with a context in mind because viewers and potential customers simplify things into stereotypes. This so-called "horn effect" has been sufficiently studied and was originally described by the American psychologist Edward Lee Thorndike, who studied the perception of human characteristics by their environment. He proved that people tend to elevate a person's salient individual (negative) characteristics as a measure of their overall character.

People who are often unpunctual, for instance, are then generalized as being unreliable. The horn effect corresponds to the human striving for orientation and simplicity. Prejudices work the same way.

Accordingly, companies or individual service providers should be careful about their visibility. Visibility in unfavorable contexts, we like to call it "toxic visibility," follows precisely these mechanisms. Individual elements of visibility are summarized by viewers to stereotypes – when in doubt even into negative ones. The previously mentioned halo effect is the opposite of the horn effect. The metaphor of an actual halo has become quite well known because "halo" also implies "outshining": positive characteristics that were just once firmly associated with a person are subsequently and immovably assigned to them. The same goes for companies, brands and influencers. In the latter case, the halo effect is also seen through very critical eyes and examined in scientific discourses. They have great authority over their followers. Since they gain visibility in a specific niche and also gain great interpretive power over their (oftentimes young) followers, influencers are frequently and unconsciously perceived as authorities.

The halo effect turns followers into uncritical people. The positive aspects that are invariably linked to the adored influencer outshine any possible criticism of the recommended product or behavior.

Customers reduce the information they have gathered about a person, company, product or solution. This is a real eye-opener for companies since it is so counterintuitive. Companies always want to offer their potential customers a lot of information – they can reveal a lot about their solutions and try to convince said customers with as many arguments as possible.

The more information companies offer their customers, the more the latter will turn the given information into simple patterns. The customer's attention is like a burning glass for information: the more light that hits the burning glass (that is, visible product information), the more it will accumulate to a single point. Thus, companies need to take this reduction process into their own hands. They have to decide which messages the information will establish in the customer's mind.

For companies, authority can be this burning glass of customer attention. It has the power to direct it and to, thus, determine which piece of information is essential regarding the company or service provider – at least to the customer's perception which decides on purchases.

Authority has the power to achieve a high level of interpretative competence. This, in case of doubt, also overcomes many challenges that the companies are not happy about when customers view their products.

Even if the products work in regards to their problem-solving features and even if people are uncritical, it is a problem for companies when customers examine it too closely: potential customers do not have unlimited amounts of time for either skepticism or the testing of products. Yet, at the same time, customers want clarity, because they fear making a mistake by purchasing the product. In conclusion, the longer the verification process, the more the potential sale is at risk.

Authority can bridge this gap and give customers the wanted security. Authority draws strength from this interpretational sovereignty and the guiding of attention.

Strong brands can make good use of this interpretive sovereignty – one of the most important reasons why companies should strive for niches in which to establish strong visible brands. Beiersdorf, for instance, has a comparatively low brand value, but their Nivea brand is a top brand in skin care. The brand takes its authority from time, visibility and long-standing trust. Such brands then become synonymous with their application, they become a general brand: "Do you have a Kleenex for me?", "I'll quickly hoover it up" and "let's google that." These authorities are embedded so strongly in people's minds that their brand name is now synonymous with a whole product type. Now, competitors cannot get around these authorities – and even if, then only with maximum effort.

With other products, the interpretational sovereignty is even greater. As soon as Apple brings out a new iPhone, all competitors look to them as the market-defining authority. They know that Apple products are automatically elevated to an industry standard. If you want to compete, you have to be better than Apple – it is not only a matter of surpassing the brand in terms of product attributes, but of doing it so well that the barely expungable disadvantages become irrelevant in your own brand perception. Yet, Apple interprets relevance from its lofty position as brand authority: precise, reduced design, shatterproof glass displays or wireless headphones, for instance. This is another way of recognizing authority, and it is what makes this status so desirable – none of these features are actually relevant to the product benefit for making a simple phone call.

Finally, an interesting distinction: there is a big difference between authority and authoritarian behavior. Some teachers excel in authority, they are quiet and calm, do not have to state consequences or argue at length why students should or should not do something. Still, students follow their rule gladly and are eager to learn. They impart knowledge by virtue of their authority.

Other teachers have to do the exact opposite. They threaten with consequences, use authoritarian means, get loud and give out penalties. They are the worse teachers.

However, visibility always has the following guideline at its core: potential customers decide of their own volition whether or not to pay attention to visibility – they can switch channels or look away at any given time. Visibility is always subject to the recipient's gratuitousness. Thus, companies almost inevitably fail if they do not seek genuine authority in regards to their customers.

Ultimately, authority also determines the stories that people listen to and believe.

Visibility can be retained through storytelling over long periods of time – while coincidentally building a brand

If a product's or service's relevance can be guaranteed for the customer, and if it is also certain that the provider has the necessary authority over its customers in its guidance function, then the business owner who wants to sell something is only left with the need for a good story.

Relevance and authority are strong pillars of smart visibility, which is more valuable and rarer than worthless visibility, yet easy to produce if you know how to. However, relevance and authority by themselves are immovable qualities; for effectivity, they need a vehicle or means of transport to get to the customer. Companies without visibility rely on chance, on customers finding them by accident and then experiencing the company's relevance and authority. In doing so, however, companies leave far too much to coincidences.

Imagine it like vital nutrients in the body that cannot get to the cells without a catalyst. Storytelling takes on the catalyst function for your business, thus, securing sales successes. Stories are the catalysts for visibility.

Sticking with this metaphor for a bit, stories transport not only information, relevance and authority. As in the cells with nutrients, there

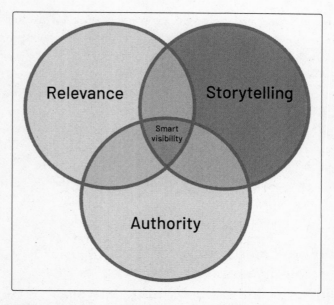

Storytelling complements the dimensions of relevance and authority.

Source: original illustration

is a deficiency of information. People want good information and actively look for it, so if these contents are available in an intriguing, condensed form, then they will get to the customers as if by a sort of magic. Good stories do all that.

Two ideas are especially helpful in understanding storytelling: the first is the one of the seven contact points in sales. In marketing, there is a popular belief that a customer needs seven contact points with the product to then decide to buy it. This is linked with the fact that customers want to check out products, that it may not meet them with the necessary temporal relevance at the first contact or even that its content may not (yet) have the appropriate relevance for them.

However, it may also be linked to the fact that the supplier was not yet able to build up sufficient authority toward these customers during the earlier contact points. With every contact, potential customers learn more about both product and company. This may lead to an increase in their trust, leading to a growing inclination to buy. With these seven contact points, it is therefore valuable if the information conveyed to customers at one contact point would still be present at the next – otherwise companies have to start all over again each time.

> Essentially, storytelling is about storage processes between individual moments of visibility and the permanent communication of information. Stories store visibility. At the same time and almost incidentally, they build up the company's brand.

By the way, probably the most unimportant aspect about the "seven-contact rule" is the number itself. Some products need more contacts, others less. Impulse purchases may already happen after only one contact but rarely with high prices or margins; some other products such as capital goods, as for instance a complex production line, may only be sold after the 15th contact. Either way, it is important to know that a sale usually takes several contact points.

The second helpful idea is derived from the question of why people remember stories particularly well. Many an epic, for instance, has been handed down for generations, from antiquity to the present day, has survived empires and cultural circles – in some cases even without a written tradition. These stories were not found on an ancient papyrus that had been dug up and rediscovered after 2,500 years, instead, they were told by word of mouth over millennia. The story of Oedipus, the *Odyssey* or parables from the Bible are still gladly told today and almost anyone could give a rough outline of most stories. Sometimes it is only single narrative patterns or a story's particularly strong parts that are handed down this way. There is a phenomenon behind this persistence of stories that is linked to humans' memory capacity:

Often, we can remember stories better than sheer facts. We prefer listening to stories than to just information, and we like repeating them to others. Stories have a privileged access to consumers and often exhibit aspects of viral marketing: they are retold, for instance, as anecdotes.

So stories are indispensable when we talk about retained visibility which customers are meant to remember after several contact points and which are meant to attract reliable attention through emotions at every contact point.

Stories live off emotions

The main reason why stories are remembered particularly well is their relatable emotions, which people like to engage with and which they can grasp and interpret both competently and quickly. Stories take readers or viewers on a journey, portrayed emotions are empathically experienced by listeners, while images that make up the story are well remembered.

It is like a great holiday that you always fondly look back on. With such memories, information also often takes a back seat to emotion. You may have after only a short time after your return home forgotten the name of the hotel or your room number – they no longer have a guidance function.

Yet, one particular story sticks: it is the one with the pleasant Italian grandmother who offered you tomatoes from her own garden as you were walking along, and they tasted so incomparably like tomatoes as you have never tasted before, no supermarket could ever offer such a taste. And suddenly information is also stored in your memory: "Nonna" means grandma, for instance. Why did that stick? It is a well-known fact that stories with strong emotions remain stuck fast in your memory.

Stories retain information over long periods of time

The Ancient Greeks are still known to this day, among other things, for having invented democracy. One of its important elements was the people's assembly, the *polis*, of which the concept of politics is derived from. Then, as now, politics included a plenum for the exchange of arguments and the making of flaming speeches for the preparation or criticism of decisions. The Ancient Greeks made these speeches with great emphasis, and they put a lot into motion in order to be convincing. Their most effective means of doing so was the art of rhetoric. One important element of it was the free deliverance of a speech in front of the plenum.

In ancient Greece, writing was long frowned upon, as it was said to threaten people's ability to remember. Those wanting to give a really good speech to the plenum needed to memorize a speech that could be several hours long, and the best way was through stories – it was considered an art form. For this purpose, the Greeks used the method of a "memory palace": they imagined their daily walk to the plenum, where they wanted to give a speech, so they placed individual speech elements in their imagination on the way there. If that day's speech was to be a call to war, then perhaps in their fantasy journey they placed the body of a killed enemy soldier on the temple's first step. Such images are easily memorable and, above all, do so for a very long time.

The speakers used this technique image by image to memorize many key words for their speeches and then derived the spoken manuscript from them. It was important that the images were emotionally strong, thus, easy to remember.[5]

Stories, which ideally stimulate emotions, can achieve something that must be worth a lot to most companies in regards to their promotional messages: stories can convey many facts without it being taxing for customers to remember them. This increases the likelihood that customers will remember the information, as does the likelihood that customers might even be happy to share the stories with others after having felt a strong emotional connection.

Companies are given a wonderful catalyst for information that they can sent to their customers. Ultimately, it is about conveying facts and arguments to potential customers, which they can then use to make their purchase decision.

The intelligent use of stories circumvents the fact that potential customers have little desire for mere information. They do want to use it for their decision, to check relevance and authority, but they still know that all this involves work and research. This puts the deal in jeopardy –

perhaps the customers would rather decide against a deal than regret it later – which makes it so important to present them with the decision-making tools through nice stories.

> Stories are to information as liverwurst is to the dog's deworming treatment: if you hide the information well in them, it is gladly taken, even if the actual information is not that attractive. Later, it can then also unfold its effect on the customer.

Overall, stories are a sheer dream in regards to the visibility of product benefits. So the derivation from the second idea about the function of stories is that emotions, like catalysts, can transport and reinforce the information they contain.

To see the full significance of this possibility, we only have to consider the effort it takes for a prospective customer to remember a great product's five most important sales arguments – listed emotionlessly in a table. Obviously, customers try to avoid this sort of effort. It takes a good deal of enthusiasm to remember a car's technical data, for instance, over a longer period of time – and cars are still some of the more emotionally charged products out there. It is a completely different story with everyday items like washing-up liquid or hairspray. These products have to fall back on emotional content to make a connection.

The art of telling stories is as old as mankind. It has lost none of its importance even in times of digital information and a plethora of advertising messages.

Today, storytelling is increasingly seen as one of the magic words of marketing. This goes so far that, for instance, the local chambers of industry and commerce or other local business associations are now keeping a watchful eye on this trend, offering informative events and training courses on it.[6] This way, storytelling is being transferred from the marketing avant-garde to the daily work of local companies.

It is no longer the big global players like Apple, made famous for instance by the product presentations of the iPhone or the iPod as events full of strong stories, that make the difference with storytelling. For quite a while now, smaller companies have also been looking at how to improve their marketing with storytelling.

This can bring them a competitive edge since storytelling is not yet seen as a lucrative marketing strategy by many small and medium-sized companies, but it works very well and is rather inexpensive. Due to the fact that many companies are yet to discover good stories for their marketing, consumers are still willing to pay attention to the existing stories, and they are still on the lookout for stories – unlike traditional, merely promotional content.

And should you still be doubtful about the effect of stories and how they can be used, then please ask yourself the following questions:

1. Which effect does mere information have without a story? Which contents were shown in the last PowerPoint presentation of 80 slides that you were allowed to listen to last? Please name five facts and insights you still remember from that. Or please list your food processor's performance data, or that of your drilling machine or any other appliance you like to use frequently. So you see, mere information that is not linked to stories is very fleeting.
2. Why are they called "stories" on Instagram, WhatsApp and Facebook? Because people want to tell their stories and want to see stories! These channels are very successful and essentially tell little stories.
3. Why are some really outlandish products with a great story being sold successfully? Because people have a great heart and tend to listen to stories that are sometimes more worthwhile than the product itself.

You still cannot believe it? Well, then please check out "Pet Rock." It is a stone sold as a pet for all those who want to take on less responsibility. It can be bought, for instance, on Amazon in the States for about 20 dollars. What you get is a stone in a paper cage with a bit of hey, like a real pet. Certainly, the joke is the biggest part of this product for those who buy it as a present or hand it out to visitors, since the product's actual use, to put it mildly, is rather limited. Still, Pet Rock grossed at over 1 million dollars in its first year of sales.[7]

Yet, stories have proper advantages as well. It has become increasingly expensive and unsuccessful to produce a large coverage, especially in scattering marketing. Television and radio spots cost a lot of money, large advertising campaigns in national magazines are expensive. All the worse if you then fail to make a difference with your message. It is much more effective to produce inexpensive marketing that transports valuable messages to the most exciting customers, even without costly coverage.campaigns and scattering advertising.

Stories have exactly this power. Stories arouse emotions, convey information and can even cover up a product's weaknesses.

Which is your authentic story?

Initial costs of good stories are basically your imagination and understanding of your offer. Since they are so interesting for customers, they will quickly take on wings of their own and will need much less expensive print marketing to get them past the threshold of customer attention.

For this to work, companies just need to know their own unique story and the aspects that make customers listen to them. Admittedly, this is time-consuming because it requires a different view on how to market your own company's abilities – and might even need a new vision of your company and its products. Yet, this is feasible if you incorporate it into tried and tested narrative patterns, for instance, the pattern of a long-standing tradition in combination with historical places people long for, such as Normandy or Tuscany, as Acqua Panna proves.

Stories are also something like a sorting aid for the actual business work. Imagine it like a child who is asked to sort through the toys it has left lying around while playing. If you say to the child: "Tidy up your toys!", this seems to be a difficult task to accomplish – even so difficult that it will refuse to do so. Yet, if you ask the child to sort the toys according to their colors and put them in respective boxes, for instance, or to put the toy cars in one box and the dolls in another, then the child quickly has an idea of how to proceed. The task is now easy because it has become clear.

AN AUTHENTIC GIFT OF NATURE

Filtered drop by drop through the hills of Tuscany, untouched by man, Acqua Panna natural mineral water is a gift of nature, with a heritage dating back to 1564.
It is also an actively preserved symbol of Italian refinement and taste, savored the world over, at the table and on the go.

A PERFECTLY BALANCED TASTE

Naturally crafted by the Tuscan nature and bottled directly at the source, Acqua Panna is renowned for its unique flavor profile. The mineral composition is behind its unique taste and makes it a favorite with sommeliers, chefs and discerning consumers worldwide.

Even water can have a background story: the Nestlé Group's luxury mineral water Acqua Panna weaves historically and emotionally charged words such as "Tuscany," "Florence" and "Domus Medici" into the water's story – the year 1564 emphasizes this effect. In Germany, a liter of Acqua Panna costs around 1.20 euros, while Aldi's own brand, Quellbrunn, goes for 0.13 euros per liter. In comparison, this makes Acqua Panna over 900 percent more expensive.

Source: Nestlé Marktplatz (https://www.acquapanna.com/intl/)

Currently, companies face a similar challenge, but they cannot solve it so easily in most cases. From their deep understanding of it all, they could tell anyone interested an infinite amount about every business ability and every one of their products; they also know the products' every single advantage and every supposed customer benefit. However, companies have little overview of their own true abilities, their offers' best customer benefits and the customer needs, precisely *because* they know their products too well!

People rather listen to Brian Cox and Robin Ince[8] who invite guests and explain science phenomena in layman's terms in their BBC program *The Infinite Monkey Cage*. Listeners then think they might have a better grasp on the universe and its effects than if they had just read a science book about it. True, the book will go more into depth on certain aspects and topics and will probably also be more nuanced in its explanations, yet, it will still reach less readers and will, effectively, have brought less knowledge into the world.

The amount of information is actually an obstacle to its distribution because the stories make the difference, not the abundance of information. Sometimes, this might even be detrimental.

A reduction of detailed corporate knowledge and the versatility of corporate abilities to just clear and structured but catchy stories can take on a valuable organizing function. This is true both for the companies themselves, who can then view their products from a new perspective and communicate the benefits more clearly, and for the customers, who want to understand the product just as clearly.

How is a customer supposed to find product benefits and connection points if not even the company can define them precisely? Many companies (but also individual entrepreneurs) find it difficult to give a one-sentence elevator pitch on their offer. They could explain it convincingly in an hour, but who would listen to it all?

Customers are not particularly motivated and do not look for connecting points on their own initiative. They briefly devote some of their rare attention to the product in order to then decide whether this product seems obvious enough. Should this not be the case, then they might, if worst comes to worst, buy a competitor's product that was communicated more clearly with more vivid stories – or nothing at all. Seems unfair? Maybe.

Customers do not tend to buy the best product, and they do not tend to buy from the superior company in the market either. Customers might buy the second- or even fifth-best product – in any case, they buy the one they understand best. They buy the product with the best story, the one whose features and benefits are presented to them vividly and to which they can clearly link their expectations of the product solution.

Stories structure communication of corporate abilities both internally and externally. They have a faster impact, are more attractive and better create a lasting effect. Companies with no understanding of story-telling, who think the criterion of relevance is sufficient, i.e. who do not try to create this form of visibility with their customers via stories, are thus at a considerable business disadvantage.

Bringing stories to life and embedding them

In addition to their structuring function, as shown above, emotions also have an important function for story effectiveness. Today's television viewers, Internet users or newspaper readers encounter many adverts and their messages. Studies indicate that these add up to several thousand pieces of advertising content per day and person. It should now be immediately obvious that this is the neuralgic point of advertising regarding its visibility. Standing out amongst thousands of competing pieces of information is advertising's first step to business success. At the same time, it is also the key challenge. Visibility just by itself is almost worthless.

So, if stories can structure corporate communication both externally and internally, and can plausibly communicate product benefits to potential customers, then this would mean that only the customer's initial attention needs to be caught. Well, with emotions or a good, surprising momentum, that can easily be achieved with stories.

Emotion is a privileged key to the art of attracting attention from potential customers. Yet, they are often less easy to tie to products or services. Tying a washing machine, for instance, or an entire DIY store to emotions does not really suggest itself.

Fortunately, receivers want to connect to the sender's emotions and are always on the lookout for them. Plus, they are highly competent in terms of empathy, so they recognize emotions in seconds, not least because in real contacts we also depend on classifying the emotions of someone else within the shortest time possible – that is certainly an evolutionary and now social success factor.

Thus, emotions have a good chance of generating visibility in general. While watching a commercial's storyline, viewers cannot help themselves but read the protagonists' emotions quickly and nearly stereotyped. Just like particularly strong positive or negative emotions could be memorized well in the memory palace, it can also be assumed that they stand out well in such a flood of content. Emotions not only anchor and store visibility but also quickly and early attract the potential customer's attention, whom the abundance of information and advertising has otherwise taught well on how to ignore them.

By the way, this is also the case in real life: someone on the tube will notice first and foremost the smiling or crying faces – after having looked at a sea of stoic faces. Even just yawning or grinning broadly will automatically make you the center of attention. This can be done in mere seconds and without a doubt.

So, advertising can make wonderfully easy offers for emotions and use their strong binding power as well as the fact that they are quickly read and interpreted by people. Even with animals or objects, viewers are competent in detecting and interpreting the depicted emotions.

If you ask people about the commercial that was on tele yesterday right before daytime news, they tend to have a hard time answering this. Normally, they are too indifferent to commercials, and the mass of rather equally insignificant content was too great – adding to the lacking relevance in terms of time and content. The visibility of content is often fleeting and not retained. However, we can certainly ask about some commercials. Ask people: do you know the Meerkat from "Compare the Meerkat"? Or: do you know that special commercial which Volkswagen ran a few years back during the commercial break at the Super Bowl, "The Force"? Viewers remember such outstanding spots that arouse certain emotions like annoyance, amusement, sadness or affection or similar strong emotions.

Samsung has released an attention-grabbing commercial. It takes place in Africa, with an ostrich going about its normal life with its fellow ostriches. It is searching for food and notices a house with a table inside. Human food scraps can be seen on the table, so the ostrich begins to pick them.

Apart from the food scraps, there are also VR (Virtual Reality) glasses on the table and they accidentally slip over the bird's eyes.

The ostrich cannot shake them off and they turn on, to then show pictures of a flight above clouds from a first-person perspective, underlaid by Elton John's song "Rocket Man."

After the initial shock, the ostrich begins to look at these pictures increasingly joyfully and starts to imitate the flight movements in the African savanna. The music becomes faster and more motivating, it supports the audience's emotional involvement in the scene. The dream of flying, which many people also share and which represents a connectable emotional stereotype, becomes palpable. Obviously, the ostrich starts to get the desire to also be able to fly.

The interpretation of this is left to the viewer's imagination and empathy, but it works really well and, above all, fast. The emotions catch the viewer's attention quickly. We feel sorry for the flightless bird who repeatedly tries to take off, yet, stumbles and falls, but still watches the images from the VR glasses even at night, to then dream of flying.

After one of the next cuts, the bird actually manages to take off, watched in disbelief by its fellow ostriches. The end of the commercial has the only reference to Samsung or its products when the advertising slogan reads: "Do what you can't."

The spot is enjoyable and sticks in people's heads.

Stories leverage authority

Stories can take on yet another function. They create emotional anchor points for the brand behind the advertising message and can enrich the brand itself with values that are hard to convey to consumers or that the company does not even really have.

Another prime example for emotional advertisement is a commercial by the German supermarket Edeka in which an old man has invited his family over for Christmas. Albeit, his daughter leaves a message on his answering machine and tells him that they would not be able to visit him for Christmas this year. In the background, his granddaughter can be heard laughing and calling "Grandpa, Grandpa." In very strong images, with muted colors and in pale light, the grandfather looks out the window, lost in thought, and then at the greeting cards sent to him for Christmas. He is incredibly sad – at least, that is how it can be interpreted.

Here, the commercial deliberately uses familiar patterns of cinematic narration: a grey monotony outside the window, dim lights in the flat and the old man's heavy-looking, slow movements. As viewers of this spot, we are immediately drawn into the protagonist's emotional world. The grey world outside, the dim light inside and the old man's behavior – those are all stereotypes presented to viewers for interpretation, which happens swiftly and accurately.

One key aspect is especially interesting in this regard: viewers stop challenging what they are being shown. These interpretative ways and clear patterns that viewers can deduce are never really questioned by them.

If the brand were to then show product information right after, customers would be much more skeptical: "Christmas goose, 11.99 euros each, now at Edeka," for instance – people would ask themselves whether the goose could be bought at a better rate or with better quality somewhere else, whether animal welfare could be taken into account for this price and whether, with such a bargain, one would not have to be in the shop really early to get hold of one of them for Christmas.

At this point, customers rather prefer, unquestionably at that, to accept the guidance function of the story's narrative stereotypes of "sad grandpa." Where customers might otherwise critically question product features and facts, wanting to compare and be suspicious of a company obviously trying to convince them of the product attributes, the benefits and the grandiose production performance; instead, they follow the stories indiscriminately like sleepwalkers.

In the next part of the Edeka commercial, we see the old man's relatives receiving mail. They have apparently, their reactions being bitter tears and despair, received death notices – though viewers do not get to see the actual letter contents. Now, it has become a seriously sad commercial.

Quickly, all the relatives set out to pay their last respects to their father, respectively grandfather at his funeral. They travel and meet at the deceased's home. To their surprise, he then emerges from one of the back rooms and welcomes them, saying, "How else could I have brought you all together in one place?" Then, the family is seen exuberantly celebrating Christmas – together with the grandfather.[9]

This spot breaks with patterns and stands out because it elicits such strong emotions. As viewers, we empathize with the family's grief and are thrown into the same, veritable rollercoaster ride of emotions after the grandfather turns up alive and well.

Some of the viewers might even feel like they are not showing their own relatives the attention they deserve – and might feel caught out. The viewers develop these feelings from what they have seen, charge it even further and form a wide connotative space of emotions, values and points of connection. This feeling of not having contacted some relatives or friends as often as we would have liked or should have done is probably quite common – thus, builds an emotional connection. This sort of effect could never be achieved with mere product information.

However, the spot does not simply exploit and bluntly repeat the viewers' emotions. Themes of death, guilt and responsibility are not in the least typical of advertising, certainly not of advertising for consumer goods. Instead, here they are built up as a contrast to the homely and the feeling of happiness after the discovery that he has not died after all and Christmas can be celebrated together.

So, first of all, these feelings are surprising, they stand out in the advertising landscape. Second, they are strong, tied to distinct emotions that viewers can empathize with, might even be heightened by the strong contrast of sadness and joy. Third, they are still easily and quickly readable for viewers; the fact that death and grief are seldomly the subject of advertising for consumer goods does not mean that they are not easy for viewers to read, since they know them well from other contexts such as feature films or novels.

In a way, this Edeka commercial has found a niche of strong emotions that would otherwise not be part of its advertising, and it has shown a way to integrate them perfectly into the message despite the attention-grabbing internal contrast.

Thereby, the commercial fulfills another requirement of good storytelling that makes the difference in this flood of advertising content: it surprises by breaking with expectations. When thousands of advertising messages pelt consumers on a daily basis, surprise must be the order of the day.

First the story, then the product

Products play a very subordinate role in this spot, they are brought onto the table during the Christmas dinner, rather en passant. Instead, it is the emotions that are being conveyed here, celebrating Christmas with loved ones and taking one's time for the family, wanting to invest in them.

This way, Edeka manages to use the story to charge its own image with emotions – something a mere product description could never have done. Edeka suddenly stands for responsibility toward the family, for a "homely feeling" and for the security of doing the right thing in hectic times – as well as love and attention. This must also be noted as a feature of good storytelling: the brand takes a back seat to the emotions and the offer of emotional and moral connection with the content – only to then benefit from it all the more. Quiet instead of loud is the key.

It is a sensible reaction to the flood of loud, annoying advertising content indicated before, which otherwise tends to burden consumers. The mere enumeration of product features and a list by the manufacturer of the product's advantages no longer work for today's consumers – they cannot. People compare, are suspicious and look for their own approaches to the qualities of brands and products. In the end, they are rarely interested in the product itself, but rather in the goals they can achieve with it, the values and emotions they associate with it, and often also what they communicate to their surroundings with this purchase.

Yet, companies still report too often in their marketing on means to achieve goals but far too rarely on the fact that they are desperate to achieve these goals *with* their customers – which would make the customers' goals their own.

Again, this is a function that stories can perform: they can leverage factors that customers may associate with products but would be unlikely to do so based purely on product descriptions. Clever storytelling can multiply these factors as if out of the blue.

Imagine shopping in a normal supermarket right before Christmas, with all its stress, maybe add to that the rows of shelves and the situation at the till. This might remind you again of how this time feels less like the tear-jerking feeling of "at home" or "one's connectedness with the family." Only the commercial and its storytelling created this feeling and links the brand to moral values that would otherwise be hardly achievable for it. This approach basically solves two problems simultaneously: on the one hand, they found a way to advertise their products without having to line up one argument after another. And secondly, they succeed in attaching values to their products that would hardly be attributed to them per se – thus making the brand highly attractive.

Since these values are woven into a comprehensible story with the right balance between invoking familiar narrative patterns and a surprising momentum, the viewers perceive this visibility as authentic and honest marketing. They are much less suspicious of the evoked feelings than if Edeka had presented certain features of the products on offer.

Stories have clearly conceivable patterns

Storytelling then takes on an awakening function by integrating strong emotions. The deliverance of these emotions makes the difference to content otherwise found in the white noise of advertising. These strong emotions, transported by the story, also create an attachment to the brand. The story can perform this transport function so well because people are used to and competent in reading such patterns quickly and confidently. Just from the relatives' reactions to the letter, the content of which viewers cannot be sure about, it becomes immediately recognizable that something has happened, and implicitly probably to the old man. This works in a split second, without an uttered or written word.

However, storytelling is such a valuable marketing factor *because* it can easily be replicated by companies. They just have to fall back on the same structures, patterns and identification factors in order to work. These patterns are also relatively easy to reproduce; storytelling only needs to develop a truly creative momentum at a few important points.

Customers are satisfied with a handful, often very similar stories. We will elaborate on this further on.

In a way, good storytelling builds a cosy lair of the familiar for its audience, while also mixing in a little surprise element, just enough to grab attention without confusing viewers.

Companies only have to ask themselves just once: what is our own story that we can inspire people with? This story must then be brought to the point and told effectively – the best stories are short. It offers customers clear contact points, which can only come from the company's clarity as to what it wants to offer to its customers.

How to use the WHW rule for your own stories

Generally, effective storytelling by companies and for products have, like the tales of the old, a hero, describe the solving of a problem and show the reaching of a goal – be it flowers for granddad, Steve Jobs or the Red Bull testimonial and extreme skydiver Felix Baumgartner. All of these act like heroes in rising to a challenge or turn the world into their own adventure playground.

The main pattern and style-shaping elements of all good stories can be listed easily enough and can then be turned into elements of your own successful storytelling. Good stories fulfill the WHW rule of good storytelling and have united these aspects:

Who acts *how* to achieve *what*?

Even with advertisement, it needs to be clear which company is the correct go-to for convinced customers later on: who is advertising? The spot of the flying ostrich might be rather difficult if Samsung had left out the sales message at the end. The customer might now be winged, so to say, to buy either VR glasses or a new television set – because they would just not know which manufacturer had opened up these fantasy worlds and is such an authority on great visual experiences.

Furthermore, it needs to be clear *what* the goal is when a customer buys the product. It needs to be perceivable *how* the product can help to reach this goal.

Earlier on we explained how information needed to take the back seat, behind good storytelling. This is still true, but information also needs to be the backbone of the story, from which the emotions, pictures and expectations of the customers can ensue. After all, stories are a means to an end: bringing both purchase decision and essential information to the customer.

As part of storytelling, these can be changed and abstracted so that they offer much more effective connection possibilities to customers. It should still be conveyed who the customer should buy the product from and what it can do, mind you, as a *solution* to customer problems or wishes.

Odysseus has to go through his adventures to return as a better person – that is the story archetype. And followers of a vanlife blogger only need to go along with his fantastic tips, purchase the recommended products to try to emulate his life. These are clear structures as well. However, a repetition of the basic structure does not necessarily mean a vapid story – quite the contrary. There needs to be more to the story, developed around a clear structure:

- The first person stepped onto the moon to follow humankind's inquiring minds and to show what technology can achieve. This has worked thanks to NASA's technological superiority.
- Bertrand Piccard managed to fly around the globe with a solar-powered plane for the first time because he wanted to prove that regenerative power is effective and reliable enough for general usage.
- Steve Jobs has led Apple to its present success because he overcame challenges and setbacks and because he trusted his fantastic entrepreneurial abilities and beliefs.

Stories and their heroes: the "who"

Good stories need identification figures: heroes. Heroes have a key advantage. They are protagonists with human traits and behavioral patterns – for instance superheroes in comics or stories such as *Star Wars*. These heroes are suitable as identification figures because they project patterns that viewers would also like to follow. They pursue goals and visions, want to be morally right with every decision and want to be successful. So, for the customers, heroes in stories are proxies. This proxy function is extremely reliable and strong: viewers at the cinema are frightened, just like the protagonist in a dangerous situation, they cling to the seat or their partner's arm. This works in fairy tales or pop songs which make the listeners cry because it is so touching. Stories quickly have this power over people, to make the listeners identify with the protagonists, to make them want to experience how the characters have overcome challenges – and they want to do so on a deeper level.

In film and television studies, this effect is called catharsis. A story's emotions like fear, happiness, love or relief are compatible and viewers partly go along with them, knowing that this sort of situation could never happen to them personally.

Yet, it is a pleasant emotional cleanse (in classical Greek: κάθαρσις kátharsis) to go along with these emotions, up to a point, mind you, and to engage with them. We neither have to fear any harm nor do we really have to fall in love or overcome any other emotional challenges – we can just taste it a little bit without being directly involved.

This is like a light running training which makes you stronger for the next run without straining yourself too much. Catharsis is one of the main reasons why we like to engage so quickly and readily with stories.

Still, for this effect to work, the story needs an identification figure who goes through the challenges for the viewers and who overcomes them. This way, the hero is the bridge between both the viewers and the emotion, but also inside the information of the story.

In storytelling, it is assumed that this hero can be represented by different protagonists.

On the one hand, this can be the company. However, we should go about this with caution because a company's overly self-indulgent portrait tends to lead to skepticism on the customer side. That would be "old marketing."

However, not the companies tell the stories, but people behind or inside the companies. This means, it is mediated storytelling mostly in which, for instance, a salesperson can talk about the fact that they are part of this company.

They could talk about how the company has taken on the great task of solving its customers' urgent problems. Since the company sends its representative forward as an enthusiastic testimonial, this automatically comes across as more serious and less self-indulgent. Still, the problem remains that an employee would never be unbiased about their company.

In comes the stylistic device of turning the customer into the story's hero.

This is how a company should talk about best-practice examples: "With our help and advice, our customer Max Miller was able to fulfill the following vision … our special approach helped him because our products can guarantee the best results." This is both the main statement and the story line.

The protagonists who are very adapt at writing about themselves in a hero story are usually freelancers, self-employed or service providers with direct customer interactions, thus, are suitable as direct identification figures.

When a story of one's own heroism is well told, it also offers an excellent starting point to embed the message visibly for customers. Obviously, a hero story should not be too self-indulgent, otherwise it will be challenged by customers.

Therefore, one of the recurring elements of such stories is the dealing with failures and challenges. Particularly, many coaches, counselors and mentors like to tell such stories in which they themselves have overcome obstacles. Such stories have a very good chance of being perceived as honest and authentic by customers.

Again, though, a company's or service provider's self-adulating advertising tends to invoke a suspicion of positive exaggeration. People with tales of their own challenges, setbacks, failure and their getting back up are often perceived as more credible.

To emphasize it once again: these are narrative clichés! From the outside, they can be attributed much more clearly, appear to be much more stereotypical and easier to see through than when they unfold their full effect as part of a good story.

We must caution against the misconception that customers would not like to take up such stories only because, from a meta-perspective, they seem transparent. Everyone experiences these stories, and when they are presented, they also unfold their effect – even if the background is well known.

Media studies calls this effect "double knowledge." Everyone knows that feature films or novels are fictitious, still, they are thrilling or emotionally touching. The same goes for stories since viewers know most of the time that they do not dive into it with rational empathy, still, they look for such stories. That is one of the reasons why we like to read crime fiction or a sentimental story on holiday; with their wonderfully told narratives, they help us escape our daily lives.

Thus, it would be an entrepreneurial disadvantage not to know, use and believe in these basic story structures. You have to make them *your* stories, though, and add relevance and authority to them.

When failure and heroes are brought together in stories, anti-heroes tend to be not too far away. They are either clumsy, blundering types who are still capable of being likable, or Robin Hood types who break the law to achieve their (albeit, honorable) goals.

Elon Musk is such an anti-hero who puts competitors in a bind because, for instance, he buys the suppliers of an entire industry to then use the products only for his own company – much to the disadvantage of others but to the advantage of *his* goals of shaking up the industry.

It is much more important to achieve goals that match those of the customers than to have a clean record as a hero, who is allowed to fail at times and has rough edges.

Stories need goals: the "what"

It is perfectly acceptable and legitimate that heroes fail in a story; it might even increase the story's authenticity. Though, this failure, like any success, must happen while trying to reach a clear goal. Failure and success are only conceivable with a goal in mind. In a story, the goal is evident and then achieved – or not. One thing becomes immediately clear: ideally, the story should have a "happy ending." Failure is fine as long as it is not the end result. A hero's story is unsuitable if they had the goal firmly in mind ... to then not to reach it.

Even with fictional formats like *Inspector Barnaby* or the German *Tatort* on television, recipients do not like this: of more than 1,000 cases, only a few handful are being sold – obviously, these stories cannot take hold.[10]

It therefore also becomes clear in regards to a company's visibility: customers want a clear goal with stories – after all, that is what they are used to. Customers want to identify not only with the story's hero but their goal. This hero has taken on an issue that is also one of the customer's major problems. And it has been solved by the hero. This parallel literally draws the recipients into the story. They want to know how the hero overcame the challenge. From the company's perspective, they should ensue in copying the hero's actions: by buying the product that will help them.

People like to infer from small to big things. "Pars pro toto" – a rhetoric figure in which a part of something is used for a generalization of the whole. This is both efficient and convenient. Though the deduction can also be incorrect, this makes human coexistence simply unfair at times – for instance, when it results in prejudices that are sometimes as practical as they are wrong. This requires a certain moral integrity from the advertisers.

Customers like to unerringly derive such a pars pro toto from stories – and like to think that something that has worked well for them once will do so more often or even all the time. If you take a group of ten people and show them ten exemplary customers, two of which have failed, then the people in the group will worry whether the same could happen to them. Yet, if the story is morally sound, companies can certainly harness this storytelling power by turning the customers' skepticism around on them, thus, achieving the best possible outcome for both sides.

Failing as a stylistic means works in relation to goals, but it must only ever be a delay of the outcome – for the sake of authenticity and credibility. No one needs or wants a product that helps them *almost* achieve their goal.

Stories guide to products: the "how"

So far, we have established that customers have high expectations for products. It is guidance, a problem solution and also a shortcut. Therefore, your product is the "how" – which can be integrated into the end of the story. So, a good story automatically leads to a product purchase – of course, only with added relevance and authority. We have already proven that stories are mere carriers.

Customers are faced with challenges that they themselves cannot overcome or only with great effort. Ultimately, this means that products only have a chance at precisely this point in time. If providers can prove that they can solve the customer's problem, then this adds value and relevance for the customer.

If providers can convey that they have the solution, one that is particularly reliable and quick, then customers might even be willing to pay more for it. And if the problem is big enough, these factors multiply and result in high(er) prices for the solution, which the company can then exhibit in its products and services.

Solutions are indispensable for stories; so the "how" can be told quickly.

Good stories are first and foremost short!

All too willingly, stories extensively use stereotypes, before-and-after comparisons, dreams, visions and many other narrative stylistic devices to carry their audience along – maybe more artfully in a Shakespearean drama but not necessarily more persuasively. All these are forms of images and visualizations.

Besides, the human brain and its memory has functioned like this for eons – even in the Stone Age, knowledge and information were preferably conveyed via stories. And they found their most timeless usage in pictures. Cave paintings from the Stone Age, depicting a few hunters slaying a mammoth, are a collection of such stories.

In them, prey and several hunters are usually depicted iconically. That just by itself has an informative value. It took several hunters to kill a mammoth. The hunters used spears and large rocks, gathered around the animal – the story of a successful hunting strategy. Who has to act how to achieve what? From today's perspective, this was a brilliant move to preserve this information in a drawing on a cave wall. This way, the information could be brought home to any novice hunter with force, but without them having to put themselves in dangerous situations of actually hunting an animal. Supported by the image, the information was both plausible and easy to remember. The individual elements have acquired a simplified, recognizable, thus, iconic character – a mammoth from one special cave of the many famous caves in southern France, for instance, is still recognizable to this day, even though they usually tend to look quite alike.

> A simplified model of a mammoth is used there, and the people are equivalent to today's stick figures, have thus assumed a more than iconic and permanently valid function as a storehouse of information. This story is one thing, and one thing only: it is short!

Since these story drawings and patterns are so simplified, viewers do the rest. If a beauty blogger, as a role model that viewers want to emulate, recommends a certain product, then the consequence is "hidden" in this tiny gap of information, which is actively filled by followers: "I have to use the product."

Viewers have always identified with these figures. Simplifying patterns are easily and readily used to put oneself in someone else's shoes.

Short stories answer short questions: how do I find a mammoth, and what do I do when I have successfully found one? How do I achieve the goal of turning it into a life-sustaining meal without harming myself?

We can well imagine how these simplified drawings could also be used for a storytelling that, quite memorably, answers these questions. Today, such stereotypes are just as much in use: success, happiness, wealth, love, security, abundance, partnership, family, adventure, to name just a few. These grand narrative patterns work amazingly well –

always. And people are satisfied with a few, simple and familiar patterns: "Are we going to watch a thriller or a love story tonight?"

Maybe, you now have a cave painting of a mammoth hunt from the Stone Age in mind as well? *That* is the power of images and stories. Just as much now as it was back then.

Why should stories be short?, you might ask. Customers cannot invest too much time in skepticism. They want guidance and clues to reassure themselves against making a possible mistake. They want to be able to decide as quickly as possible that they are doing the right thing with this product or service, that it would optimally solve their problem, and with the best price-performance ratio at that.

Many reasons – one purchase: disadvantages of well-informed customers

Companies cannot always rely on their ability to name concrete customer needs correctly – one more reason to consider stories when they want to sell something.

Obviously, companies cannot just list good arguments for a certain purchase for customers in their advertisements any longer – hoping they will then fall back on these arguments and decide on buying this product or service. There is no more guarantee that customers will trust the company's ability enough that this alone will lead to a purchase or that they will think of these abilities when looking at an advert.

Rather, customers make a wide variety of decisions when selecting a product or service, which ultimately make or break the sales success. These decisions are then based on the most diverse channels.

However, "wide variety of decisions" is a dangerous marketing goal because it is vague. And this imprecise goal describes the insecurity many companies face after they have developed a product for a market they cannot read clearly, thus, feeling as if they are stumbling around in the dark.

Many companies and freelancers are excellent at remembering their own product's or service's features. They have finally broken them down to the very last detail and are enthusiastic about its advantages, which can be tied to many features. Yet, then they experience that their customers do not seem to share their enthusiasm – for reasons fully unfathomable to them. The companies know that this product can solve one of their customers' most urgent problems, it might even be able to solve it better than all other products from the competition. Still, customers may not be all that interested in the product – or worse: they buy the other, the second-rate product.

Consequently, we have to realize that today's customers can no longer be won over by simple facts. It might even become even more difficult to convince them the more facts we use. Instead, they seek their own contact points, to a large extent from the company's visibility.

Customers today are increasingly guided by emotional, less by rational aspects before their purchase decision. Therefore, it is no longer a simple "if-then" thought sequence in which rational causality is followed by a purchase. Instead, we must understand it now as a chain of aspects, of which one part is the rational feature of a product, followed by more and emotionally loaded reasons that might be decisive. This leads to a chain of decisions – in some cases even with many branching chains.

Customers may look at the product features and interpret with their own knowledge and values, composed of comparisons with other products from supposedly objective sources, from experience and moral charge.

Now, it no longer goes:

If customers need a drill with 1,250 rpm, then they will buy this particular drill because it runs at 1,250 rpm!

Rather:

When the drill becomes visible to the customer and they then compare it and it meets their requirements and a friend has the same machine and recommends it to them and the company has a sufficiently positive reputation among craftsmen and the customer has read that the manufacturer now also works sustainably and the handle has attracted positive attention from consumer reports due to its use of only a few plasticizers ... then they will buy it ... well, maybe.

The rational product features must be recognizable and relevant to the customer. The consequences of a product feature that customers recognize for themselves, however, then form the much more exciting, often emotional "goals" that customers derive for themselves from said features – these can differ strongly from one person to the next.

Hardly anyone buys a drill because they find it so visually appealing or attractive. Many see a good benefit in being able to drill a hole in the wall if need be. That is a goal – the clear customer benefit – which in this case, however, is still very much based on features, i.e. the product's technical aspects and its characteristics. Regarding the purchase decision, it is probably of little importance to the average consumer whether the machine drills the hole at 1,000 or 1,250 rpm.

Manufacturers of such machines have these factual customer benefits in mind and can emphasize them well with data sheets or information on the drill's packaging.

Yet, even with such mundane tools like drills, it quickly becomes complex. Hobby craftsmen might buy professional drills for the two or three times a year they need to drill a hole in a wall, when in actuality these drills may last not just 10,000 holes but 100,000 thanks to their particularly high-quality bearings and motor parts. So, from a rational perspective, there is little to no reason for this purchase decision. Rather, the use of this professional device has a customer benefit that *cannot* be directly inferred. The customer may be able to show off to their neighbors with the use of such a high-quality machine. Or they may just be simply pleased in silence, drilling the three holes a year with much more motivation – "like a pro." This is a value that is linked only lightly to product attributes.

Now, "softer" factors quickly come to the fore, for instance psychological consequences of the purchase. The customer enjoys the resulting ideal customer benefit, shares it and, in turn, feels better. Customers rarely buy product attributes, instead, they buy ideas, emotions and visions. Yet, these values tend to be part of a larger story.

Take B&Q again, for instance. Their commercials have created a whole universe of values and ideas. With strong claims like "Just flip it," normal people are portrayed as jacks-of-all-trades. Normal people, after being stuck in an armchair for too long or just skipping rope, "[We] can do it,"[11] just like craftsman types with colors, handiwork and all – and tools of course.

They are overdrawn types – and are supposed to be nothing less. Stereotypes, even. This makes them icons reduced to basic patterns, almost like the cave paintings, though, now they appear in strong stories in moving images. However, there is not a single mention of product attributes in such commercials – the focus lies on the simple telling of a story. A story of people achieving goals, meeting challenges in the process and having to use all their strength and skills as well as helpful tools – these are heroes too.

Visibility in stories and the product development must be considered together

Ultimately, the end of the purchase-deciding chain is often formed by the customer's core values which they feel are reinforced by the product. The product's usage gives them a strong emotional and psychological boost with some decisions. However, these core values are often only indirectly related to the product attributes as such. That is why it is dangerous to plan, develop and optimize these attributes first in order to then create the product, *without* considering visibility in the process at all.

The purchase of an electric vehicle is a good example of such a chain of attributes and goals linked with several intermediate considerations: press coverage has made a customer become aware of it, also, the topic has been fervently discussed recently amongst acquaintances. "Electric mobility" has become a visible topic. Now, the customer is thinking about buying an electric car. Imagine this customer meeting someone at the next family party who has recently bought an electric vehicle. This often leads to an interesting development:

The e-interested person quickly seeks a conversation with the e-driver. Anyone who has ever observed or witnessed such a situation will know that there is *always* this one question: "How far is the reach of your car?" This is about a benefit, not a technical product feature, not an attribute. With the booming industry of electric vehicles, many people have even less access to precisely these technical attributes. It used to be simpler since anyone could give and understand a classification of a vehicle by stating, for instance, a petrol consumption of 8 liters per 100 kilometers – whereas now, hardly anyone has any idea whether 20 kilowatt hours per 100 kilometers are a lot or little consumption. The question of range, on the other hand, is sure to come up. It is a goal already deduced from the attributes, a clear-cut customer benefit. However, it is still an obvious, deduced benefit.

If one of the conversing participants has already decided upon buying an electric car, higher values and benefits immediately emerge that they had barely registered before: as a driver of such a vehicle, they can participate in this conversation and prove themselves to be interesting, they get attention and a higher social status. They might even be able to claim a certain expert knowledge for themselves and gain authority on the topic. That alone is an interesting goal for the electric car driver – something car engineers probably did not have in mind. A manufacturer is unlikely to argue: buy our new electric vehicle and you will be the center of attention regarding these vehicles at every social event. And yet, this could be a customer motive, a powerful one even!

Development teams hardly think that far ahead, which is precisely why car manufacturers afford themselves an engineering department *and* a marketing department (and a design department, etc.). Even marketing departments often have a hard time recognizing this far-fetched customer benefit and incorporating it into their marketing campaign. It is fair to say that many early electric car enthusiasts also bought an electric car because they could then participate in conversations – being perceived as early adopters, which in turn promises a certain (good) reputation. And because now others may appreciate them for their expertise in this field. So the electric car promises the transference of a positive image onto the driver.

Obviously, companies are well aware of these connections. It is just wrong to assume that marketing departments should only clothe the results of the engineers' activities in comprehensible and user-oriented sales messages. However, even companies like car manufacturers have found rather different ways to achieve this connectivity with the customer in stories.

For instance, Tesla vehicles have a so-called "Ludicrous Mode" built in. Yet, this is not activated automatically right from the start, instead, drivers need to activate it in one of the menus. Apart from this mode's surprisingly agile driving experience, the name alone is a cleverly constructed way for proud Tesla drivers to powerfully illustrate their car's benefits. Furthermore, "ludicrous" is deliberate and probably better than a more technical description like "high-performing."

This was clever thinking from the other end of the chain, from product features and customers' deductions – with a clear success in sales, proven by the numerous videos on YouTube, for instance, with customers proudly presenting this mode to fellow drivers and their YouTube community.

Presumably, Tesla had not set aside marketing budget for these videos but just benefited from the fact that its customers suddenly created visibility for the product. This shows the power of a good understanding of stories. It can turn pressure marketing into pull marketing, turning consumers into producers of publicity for the product, thus, generating disseminators of information on product features. In marketing, these are called "evangelists," loyal ambassadors of a product's or company's superior qualities, i.e. valuable visibility.

Perhaps, companies should ask themselves more frequently: what is our "Ludicrous Mode"? A mode of this kind pays a great deal into value-based visibility, leads to evangelists – in turn, possibly, to a viral effect of their visibility.

We can take away two important deductions from this regarding visibility: first, it must be valid to do more complex thinking about the idea of a very close connection between company abilities and customer needs – if only because of the customer's quite longish decision-making chain process. It is not longer simply the customer's needs that are met by a company's abilities, symbolized by a product – which people then buy easily enough.

It is impossible to recognize all the customer's reasons for a decision to purchase a product. It would probably be rather unlikely that they could be found in the technical details or the product specifics. Instead, these decisions are based on more or less complex processes deduced from these. Which makes it immensely important to reach visibility for the product – or even the problem-solving approach – as quickly as possible. Only that would make it possible to find out at an early production stage whether the product features (which the company is most likely to have access to during this stage) really do match customer needs. Customers will later decide *which* product features they evaluate *how* – in either case, it is better to observe than to blindly guess beforehand. The only possibility for an objective assessment is the customer's decision to buy, this assesses the overlap between customer needs and products, measurable in sales figures or at least in the number of interested parties.

It is probably here that courageous, fast-acting entrepreneurs who do not try to develop the ultimately perfect product beat many an engineering-driven professional regarding speed and market entry success as well as the conversion of market opportunities into business success.

For the vast majority of products, an initial "product market fit," which may still fall short of expectations, does not mean the end of development. Instead, further development of products can be based on customer feedback.

Therefore, if possible, companies should develop products with a certain focus on later visibility, to then quickly change to visibility toward their customers.

The second deduction must be the generation of visibility toward the customer for various connecting points of their goals and values. The highlighting of a product's technical data and parameters has now become insufficient. It is now primarily about soft factors, such as a customer's possible connection to the product, a story told by the product, which might even entice them to continue on with the story, so that they can use these elements to match the product with their own goals and values.

If it is possible to reach just a few customers which can align their needs and the resulting expectations perfectly with the production features – which gives the product the ideal problem-solving competence – then this is far superior to reaching two million followers who care about the product only as long as they see it: 1.7 seconds.

Visibility does not need to be expensive

As we have seen, mere product information has a hard time in advertising – and sometimes valuable visibility is created by companies by simply doing the right thing. Sometimes, this does not even require a marketing budget.

Tesla as an example of immense success and an almost grotesque stock market quotation can shed some light on this. The brand owes part of its success to its visibility, which is different from all other car manufacturers in the world. For instance, you will not find any Tesla commercials anywhere, i.e. bought visibility. Moreover, the brand is less present in magazines and other classic distribution channels than, for instance, established car manufacturers, most of which use up massive budgets for advertising.

Tesla also has far fewer car dealerships, and, in some cases, the cars are still sold in small backyard businesses. Even worse, Tesla's media communication is sometimes considered by the industry to be catastrophic. Not even the car quality is convincing on all levels. In 2021, for instance, Tesla was once again ranked second to last in its customers' assessment for the US-American Consumer Reports.[12] From a traditional marketing perspective, this is certainly not recommended if you want to become the most valued car manufacturer. You might think now that Tesla's competition can now sit back and relax. Well, no – Tesla is one of the most expensive car brands in the world.

The brand Tesla has a completely different visibility. It is made up of mostly stories. For instance, with his presentation of the Tesla flamethrower, the company's CEO, Elon Musk, made quite a stir. Imagine the CEO of a company like Land Rover suddenly bringing out the new Land Rover flamethrower during a product presentation, testing it live on stage. It would probably be his last appearance on stage in his function as CEO. With Tesla, it is different because it fits its grand narrative.

Cyberquad is another very interesting product made by Tesla. As an electric all-terrain quad, it is also approved for children. The Cyberquad offers even more material for stories; not to mention the fact that this product could be a good move regarding the brand's early visibility amongst young customers in the future, who can then tell their own childhood stories with their Tesla and may develop a high level of attachment.

Tesla thinks from the customer's perspective, about their children's fun, proud Tesla drivers can share their enthusiasm with their offspring, which might strengthen the connection to their children. Furthermore, there is this likable notion that it is more of a heart project for the brand, as it probably will not produce huge profit margins. It is simultaneously anarchistic, cheeky and per se different from the competition.

For Tesla, the stories have worked and given the brand another push in the direction of the system-breaking, innovative and sometimes even brash and cheeky brand perception – which might be the reason why customers trust them to finally achieve the energy turnaround regarding motor vehicles.

Elon Musk's space program also naturally underlines such perceptions, into which Tesla's customers and fans then interpret values like innovative strength, technical progress and nonconformity. A company that succeeds in snatching the leadership position in space away from NASA as well as Russian, Chinese and Indian space travel presumably has sufficient technological, innovative and daring potential to manage everything else, too.

Customers rally behind such values, and they can deduce a brand's authority from such values – as we know, one of the three leading pillars of smart visibility.

Taking a closer look at the brand Tesla, some aspects definitely tarnish its image. The company is not known for being employee-friendly, instead, its boss is known for being hot-tempered and ruthless. Moreover, an ecological sustainability of space programs is just as doubtful as the assumption that vehicles with 600 hp or factories in Brandenburg water protection areas could prove to have particularly good environmental records. Yet, the stories outshine all that powerfully and certainly play an overriding role in the general reception and visibility of the Tesla brand.

It is to Tesla's advantage that people tend to not remember these unpleasant details for long. Stories that some employee representation here or there was rejected or that a few environmentalists protested in front of the new factory in Brandenburg are generally nowhere near as strong in their emotional impact as the other stories about Tesla.

The fourth mighty W: why is visibility significant?

We can add another W to the previously mentioned WHW (who, how, what), one that is considered to be particularly effective with Generation Z.

This additional building block is the elaboration of the corporate "why," a meaning or purpose: why does a company do what it does? How can the product improve the world?

In his book *Find Your Why*,[13] author Simon Sinek claims that customers always buy the "why" from companies. According to him, customers do not so much buy a company's product or even its downstream attributes, instead, they buy something that is only very loosely linked to the actual product attributes.

This statement is a culmination of all the doubts we have so far attached to the simple connections between product benefits and purchase, between company abilities and customer needs as well as between company communication and market opportunities.

Then why do companies not simply describe their why? The answer is as simple as it is startling: most companies do not even know their "why."

Most companies tend to have little problem in explaining what they do. It is, after all, their key business. Companies produce certain products, service providers solve certain customer problems and consultants provide certain advisory services in specialized fields.

However, the biggest gap for companies becomes apparent when it comes to their why. Why do they produce screws? Why did they become energy consultants? Why did they start a cleaning company? Why should you buy from them? Why are they better than others? Why are they more expensive than competitors?

This becomes clearly visible on websites of companies or service providers. A lot of space is granted to the questions who, what and how. Subpages and headlines such as "Our company," "The team," "Company history," "Portfolio," "Our consulting process in 3 steps" and many similar contents often describe the WHW – quite safely and in much detail.

The why, however, is usually missing altogether.

Sir Richard Branson is a very well-known entrepreneur. He started with a successful music label, to which he later added many other companies. Primarily, he is known for his airline. So you could call Branson the head of a record label or an airline. However, when looking up images of him online, you will find Branson appearing completely differently from, let's say, the head of the German Lufthansa. The latter is depicted in almost all pictures with suit and tie, a serious, thus, stereotypical image of a company executive.

Branson, on the other hand, can be seen in a space suit on board one of his rockets, parachuting or in other adventurous situations.

"Screw it, let's do it!", to quote Richard Branson.

There is one thing that sets Richard Branson and his company Virgin apart from others: they are set on a specific mindset and company motto which they project clearly. Richard Branson has become (in)famous for often founding new companies.

Branson holds several world records in sporting disciplines, is known for exalted April Fool's jokes – he had a hot air balloon shaped like a UFO fly over London in 1989 – and, through several channels like stories, interviews and forms of corporate communication, tells of his approach of always being happy to launch a venture to make waves in this particular industry. Or he talks about his start-ups in new niches – and of having been successful with them.

Should one not be successful then it is part of his business philosophy to not despair over it but to just tackle new adventures with at least the same amount of entrepreneurial courage. His nimbus is basically built on the fact that he is often very successful in doing just that. Branson is regarded as a daring doer who achieves his goals more often than not.

Great opportunities for identification can be found with this why, not least with the company's charismatic boss who, in his own particular way, pursues the adventurous goals of different ventures. The questions of who, what and how tie in with the why – and they do so quite easily and naturally. In particular, Richard Branson's why or that of other successful companies – at Apple, it has long been "Think different" – is representative of the idea of boldly challenging other companies and entire industries with one's own company.

With its products, Apple has quite destructively shaken up the mobile phone industry. Such companies bind certain values to themselves that would otherwise be difficult to put in a marketing promise: innovative strength, adventurousness, a departure, with top performance.

Prada's Re-Nylon answers the question of the Why

A while ago, the luxury fashion label Prada started an initiative in its own production to improve the use of nylon fibers with a more sustainable alternative, and forthwith told the customers about the "why": a more sustainable, healthy world. From the perspective of visibility, this is not without its dangers, so it is worth a closer look.

The concept of sustainability is complex because, on the one hand, companies repeatedly bend and stretch it in various directions. Despite or precisely because of its wide definition, the production of sustainable products has become a readily claimed quality feature for companies that, depending on the test's accuracy and parameters, are by no means always able to keep this claim.

On the other hand, sustainability is a very zeitgeisty term. It promises marketing advantages at a time when customers are making purchase decisions based on their ecological footprint.

Prada as a brand stands for luxury fashion items, which are usually not suspected of being particularly sustainable in the stereotypical, simplistic sense. Luxury tends to be associated with waste, fashion in general with throwaway items and production conditions are viewed critically. This could prove to be a good example of false, dishonest marketing that turns against the brand.

Due to such products, which claim zeitgeisty labels for themselves to court customers, an interesting sort of friction often emerges between brand communication and customer perception. This stands in connection with the fact that nowadays customers want to fall less victims to the brand, instead are increasingly becoming mature analysts of marketing and brands.

For this balancing act, Prada has entered into a partnership with the textile yarn manufacturer Aquafil and asked them to produce a regenerated nylon yarn made from recycled and cleaned plastic materials, fishing nets and textile fibers collected in the sea. This sounds suspiciously like "greenwashing," the phenomenon in which companies take pride in a few characteristics of sustainable and ecologically responsible behavior, hoping that customers would categorize them accordingly.

This is quite the dangerous thing to do for a brand. Some fashion labels have harmed their own image with their own weak labels of sustainable fashion that were then criticized heavily by environmental associations and consumer advocacy organizations. So, if Prada follows a similar path, then that goes hand in hand with the danger of generating visibility for objectionable product characteristics – the effort would turn against the company's marketing. Furthermore, said visibility would not be valuable, instead, it could turn toxic.

A luxury goods manufacturer with a sustainable label could be an example of misguided marketing. However, Prada is treading this dangerous field with several right steps.

First of all, Prada's persistence of implementing the use of this new material is interesting. The company has declared its goal to replace all its nylon fibers with this recycled fiber in the future. After all, they could have just done this with one or a few products from an alternative sustainable production line to appeal to customers who value this feature highly – while the other customers could have continued in not caring less. However, this corporate decision makes it seem credible and upright; this can be perceived as a mark of honest marketing.

This has a deeper impact on the company structures since the company wants to change all nylon products, and because Prada definitely places an emphasis on its production of such products. Indicating a strong commitment to this higher goal and the question of their "why," which has little to do with a bag's actual product benefits.

Even more remarkably, Prada rendered this message into a marketing campaign. First, they found a strong ally in National Geographic. Since 1888, this renowned US-American nonprofit organization has been concerned with communicating about anything regarding geography. For this purpose, researchers and their projects are supported worldwide, knowledge is imparted and, last but not least, their magazine *National Geographic* is the flagship of it all.

Additionally, videos are produced in very high quality. Prada has begun producing costly and elaborate films on all five continents with some of the society's employees, which portend to the dangers to our ecosystems and habitats – all under the label of Re-Nylon by Prada. The protagonists are actors, journalists and employees.

Prada's corporate sense has changed: its products are now focused on "planet," "people" and "culture," so the company claims. At the same time, Prada sees itself as a "driver for change."

Source: prada.com

This way, Prada is actually overfulfilling its claim to advertise its own products, though, customers appreciate it. Instead of creating 30-second TV commercials, costly reports from five continents are offered that show how sustainability is implemented there. Sometimes it is more closely linked to Prada's products and its approaches to sustainability that go into the products, and sometimes it is not: recycling, the threat of plastic fishing nets in the world's oceans and much more. The topics are not always comfortable, and they break with the tradition usually linked to luxury fashion brands. That seems honest.

Such a great effort invites viewers to identify Prada with a value core as a sustainable brand – more than a cheap reference of "Made from sustainable raw materials" would in a commercial.

The reports from five continents make a good story with several chapters. Interested customers who deal and perhaps identify with this topic can immerse themselves in a small cosmos of information, content and impressions. Plus, access to honest content, authorities and stories is offered in many places. The reporters from *National Geographic* or the Slovenian producers of sustainable materials give real-life testimonials for the values that the brand now wants to attach to itself.

Additionally, the brand can, to quite a high degree, take a back seat because, most importantly, the story transports values for them.

How to write your own story

Structures of good stories are very much alike. Entrepreneurs can orientate themselves by them, thus, have a guiding principle for the development of their own story.

In previous chapters, we have taken a look at the basic structure of effective stories. This practical part is now meant to add more interesting and concrete contact points.

A story can be constructed from five parts:

1. At the beginning, there is the so-called exposition. Here, the story's protagonist is introduced as well as the setting regarding both time and space. Many Hollywood films begin with a helicopter flight over a large American city, then there might appear a washed-up policeman in his everyday life and the remaining images reveal the time it is set, the so-called "story time." The Who, Where and When is explained here. Furthermore, basic information of the story is shared, thus it is called the establishing shot.

2. This is followed rather quickly by the so-called "plot point." The protagonist is confronted with a challenge or a crisis, or has to embark on a journey. From this point on, the tension or at least the dynamic of the narrative usually increases. Which it continues to do until it reaches a preliminary climax; a corpse is discovered, so the murderer must be found. In the following, the plot then ratchets up, for instance, through the search for the perpetrator in a crime film, or, in a drama, the protagonists are kept from pursuing their visions due to one or even several difficulties.
3. The preliminary climax is an initially logical solution to the problem. In a crime film, for instance, a first suspect is found and gets arrested after the hero's (the inspector) exciting journey, forming the first climax, which at the same time often means a first relaxation for the audience.
4. Then follows a classic so-called delay. The arrested suspect can prove to have an alibi; a new lead opens up that makes the story even more dicey. The obvious first solution was apparently not correct, so the protagonist sets out for the final decision.
5. And this final decision turns out to be the story's resolution. It is also interesting to know that, depending on the story, this can go two ways: it ends either in a drama, in the so-called catastrophe, or gets a solution with a "happy ending," usually in comedies. Traditional Hollywood cinema seems to have become obsessed with bringing very exciting and dramatic paths to a good solution.

These structures are deeply entrenched in our collective consciousness, and we were socialized with them. They are anchored in the brains of cinema visitors, TV viewers, novel enthusiasts, thus, all sorts of product consumers. Prospective customers are highly predisposed to follow such stories and are competent in reading these patterns. Stories even for the youngest start with the exposition: "Once upon a time ..." And mostly get a happy ending: "And they all lived happily ever after."

Like any story, a cinema film always needs a certain amount of abstraction. Obviously, the gangster in the film cannot harm someone sitting in the cinema, looking at him on the actual screen. And yet it is indispensable to be empathically engaged with the story to take advantage of the "double knowledge" effect that is so important for pleasant thrills. We know that the story will not have an immediate effect on us, but we love to get involved and emotionally follow the protagonists' journey. It is no different with love stories.

In turn, this effect of mental and emotional participation imprints the audience's perception with patterns. Just as you might turn around twice more than usual when walking down a dark alleyway on your way home after watching a horror film, advertising content can build such patterns with a good story. The fragrant Sunday rolls from the commercial, joyfully eaten by a happy family radiating just as much warmth as the buns fresh from the oven, are then pleasantly emotionally charged, with feelings of home, security and connection. Later, people buy these premade Sunday rolls when they feel like a little homely family time – even on their own in their student shebang.

The six levels of smart visibility

Applying value standards to marketing, Seth Godin has developed a model of six successive stages.[1]

With Seth Godin's six levels, marketing becomes more valuable with each level; the increasingly smart visibility then informs the customer about the added value.

Source: original illustration

All methods aiming at product sales can be summarized under the term marketing – therefore, economics defines it very broadly.

Seth Godin's model can be applied well and also be expanded to include the goal of incorporating visibility into the marketing process with as much value as possible. The following chapter will show how the three elements of relevance, authority and storytelling can be used together with his model, thereby being increasingly "refined" into smart visibility and successful marketing.

Level 1: Interruption marketing

According to Seth Godin, spam is the lowest form of marketing: it is associated with interrupting and annoying visibility. It only fulfills the dimensions of relevance, authority and storytelling at a low level.

Examples of this are annoying telephone calls for customer acquisition or many forms of print advertising. Clear traits of it can also be found on billboards and in television commercials as well as in those organizations trying to talk to you on the street, or with watch salesmen on beaches.

Particularly the last two examples are respected ever so little that no entrepreneur really wants to bet their reputation on them. Unfortunately, many companies still do this. Businesses often fail to see that their marketing shows clear features of spam – overlooking better opportunities as a result. Then visibility becomes annoying: "May I talk to you for a bit?" – "No, thanks, I'm in a hurry!"

All examples of spam share one characteristic: this sort of advertising garners visibility usually by contacting people without their consent, thus, violating the most important criterion of relevance. This form of advertising has such an annoying and out-of-place effect on a large proportion of people that it should really be avoided.

Still, a large portion of marketing messages has clear traits of spam and could be described, in the marketing world as a whole, as the tinnitus of sales messages – always there, annoying, yet you somehow get used to it and learn to block it out.

Its chances of success are as limited as its visibility is unlimited and ubiquitous. Therefore, it is not only unpleasant for its recipients, but it is also so encroachingly annoying and, in some cases, even needs to be regulated by law *because* of the inflationary use of such forms of advertising. This alone is a clear indicator of unpleasant consequences for advertisers: simply put, competition using this weak form of attention grabbing is getting stronger by the minute. So, in proportion, it actually promises the least success in most cases, but it is also the easiest to produce.

However, one very common, yet interchangeable and ineffective form of advertising, which companies can easily implement, is weak at its core: responses, for instance, to direct mail or mass mailings as a common means of spam advertising are usually very low in numbers. Such advertising is only ever interesting for the sender because flyers, for instance, can be printed and distributed the same day and for the smallest of budgets. Even then, the business model of gaining a few customers through this effort is tightly budgeted; usually so few customers react positively that it is barely worthwhile relying directly and solely on this method. Thus, spam marketing is no more than a weak attempt at generating a little attention, for instance, distributing untargeted advertising messages en masse with a shotgun approach.

Just like a bad shot with a shotgun may hope to hit the target sooner, albeit, with a lesser effect, so too does spam marketing sometimes land a hit. A few customers will probably buy. Otherwise, over 50 percent of all mail sent to companies and an estimated 90 percent of global email traffic would not be spam.[2]

In actuality, these are methods that companies always claim to not use themselves when asked about their visibility plan.

Be careful: even the insurance agent calling the customer in the evening is somehow close to spam – due to the offer's missing relevance. So, does that make the agent a spammer?

This honorable service provider would probably be offended if someone accused them of spam marketing – yet, objectively, this is merely a question of definition, not of bad faith. Many companies run the risk of sending out spam simply because they cannot activate any relevance, authority and storytelling for their marketing.

More than that: highly reputable spam also exists.

Actually, spam marketing is often characterized by the fact that it cannot be relevant in regards to time or content – not now and not ever. That is the second clear criterion for spam. Undoubtedly, a dog liability insurance offer is a serious product – for cat owners, though, it is still spam due to its lack of relevance.

Spam is by no means limited to digital forms of visibility: customers almost always find this sort of marketing annoying because it interrupts, for instance, their other courses of action. Someone wants to leaf through a magazine, yet, intermittently, the exciting articles are interrupted by product adverts. Or they are watching a film, yet that gets interrupted at the most exciting point for a commercial from which the TV station earns a good part of its revenue. Something else is relevant right now – and it is not the ads!

Many companies even dream of one day broadcasting a TV commercial. However, since it does not guarantee business success but is perceived as spam by viewers, which can get lost in the background noise of the eternally similar advertising messages, it is not a carte blanche for success.

An unperceived advertisement in a magazine or one of dozens of television commercials at night cannot guarantee maximum attention from viewers or readers. Why do you think many viewers go on to do other stuff during advertising breaks?

Of course, well, at least somewhat, advertisers are aware of these connections, and they know they would be well advised to overcome the customer's attention threshold with their advertising in a better way.

Using the example of the TV spot, it is particularly noticeable that scatter marketing, trying to find ways out of this dilemma, prefers, for instance, to get a slot around a time during which viewers have a high level of attention for the (other) content that they are actually watching. In this way, spam marketing tries to make itself more visible through "inherited" attention: viewers are highly attentive to an exciting film, in which a dramatic situation is now coming to a head, drawing spellbound viewers into a flow; they simply want to know what is going to happen next.

Such a scene in a film is often the "cliffhanger," a situation in which the story is about to be resolved in the dramatic climax. This is a prime advertising spot for companies – after all, they know that viewers are most likely to want to stay tuned in, so as not to miss the story ending.

For companies, the film is a Trojan horse and they try to smuggle their advertising messages in with the interesting content, hoping they will still have an effect on viewers. On closer inspection, however, this seems rather desperate. This is also the point at which the product is most likely to be accused of being spam. During the commercial break, when the film is nearing its climax, viewers will probably be the least likely to get a drink – increasing the chance of attention for commercial break contents.

Admittedly, there is no time when viewers want to be interrupted less. So they will react annoyed or even disappointed. Well, the recipients of the Trojan horse were certainly also less than pleased when they realized what they had pulled into their town – certainly not the kind of gift they had expected.

A similar logic of dressing up between exciting pieces of information is followed by leaflets in the middle of the free Sunday newspaper or are distributed by the post office neatly shrink-wrapped along with interesting bills. Usually, these are thrown away right away.

This system accepts that the majority of viewers might even be annoyed or, at best, be indifferent to the content. According to Seth Godin, advertising in such an environment is therefore the lowest level of marketing. Visibility will always have a hard time positively influencing viewers if it

- is tied to scatter marketing like direct mail, which is sent out to all of a city's households to, perhaps, catch a few interested parties;
- is interchangeable and comparable because it cannot be directed at specific customers. This violates the relevance criterion;
- breaks through really excited viewers' directed attention, like TV commercials, to attract attention.

This also applies if it fails to "pre-qualify" customers in some way, for instance, by testing or measuring their preferences to then offer personalized advertising.

Level 2: Situational marketing

Even with level 2, the customer is not specifically looking for an offer that might be redeemed by the product. By chance, however, customers become aware of the advert and it might address their needs at that moment.

This is different as temporal relevance is actually given here. The customer may look at the advert, thinking, "Look at that, what a coincidence!" – giving the offer temporal relevance. Even more so: the content's relevance is added here too. A higher level of marketing has already been reached, especially regarding the prospects of success. Still, such results are accidental, making them hardly predictable.

A typical example of such marketing are impulse purchases like the snacks in front of the checkout. The customer was not looking to buy a chewing gum or something similar just then. Also, customers do not usually go into petrol stations to buy a sports magazine. Yet, on their way to pay the petrol, it is a good opportunity for the customer to accept this offer which meets a basic need.

By the way, this is only "accidental" for customers – from the perspective of the person running the petrol station, it is very deliberate to put products exactly where they are.

Chocolate is also a good example of such a product because it often meets with consumer's low irritation threshold. Those who like chocolate and see it buy it: opportunity makes commerce. Furthermore, the price of chocolate is hardly noticeable on the petrol bill – even considering the fact that it is actually more expensive there than it usually is anywhere else. So, there are only few obstacles to the impulse.

Of course, impulse purchases also have a downside for suppliers. For one thing, it does not work with all products. The person running the petrol station would hardly be able to sell a set of winter tires or a 24-piece coffee set at this place to this person in this situation – the impulse threshold for those products is too high.

Either it is too expensive, the content-related connection to the product is not given in this situation or the customer simply lacks further contact points to be sure about the offer. Products not bought on impulse at first contact have a hard time in situational marketing.

Customers prefer to check relevance of many products – at least more than a fleeting and accidental contact would allow. This is mainly due to the brand's or seller's lack of authority. This pillar of smart visibility takes a back seat to accidental marketing, making it only slightly effective for them.

Customers are simply missing opportunities here in which they could overcome concerns, compare it with other products and appraise it from a (at least from their perspective) objective point of view. If it is a high-priced product then the risk might just be to high for customers since they are spending too much money on something they cannot yet oversee as much as they deem necessary.

Storytelling as a factor of visibility of both this product and its benefits to the customer is also severely limited. However, storytelling is the medium that can explicitly communicate product benefits to customers. Let's face it, a set of winter tires among dozens of other products in the salesroom of a petrol station does not tell a good story.

A brief look at the next steps: if the person running the petrol station were to personally approach the long-time customer and inform them that this set of winter tires near the cash register was purchased by another (retired) customer who had bought the tires but never used them, and that they were therefore in impeccable condition, then the sales pitch would be very different. Say, furthermore, the person running the petrol station, with their authority derived from years of familiarity and consistently impeccable demeanor, would also explicitly recommend these tires for this customer's vehicle, then this would add authority to the storytelling.

Albeit, authority and stories are severely underrepresented in accidental marketing – with them, marketing automatically rises to another level, more on this in a moment.

Another factor also interferes significantly: the "customer journey" is interrupted. This term is closely related to the seven-contact rule. Customers usually want to get to know the product at several points without actively feeling this need. Just as a customer would walk through a car dealership several times, taking test drives and poring over catalogs, reading automotive magazines and asking their neighbors before deciding to purchase a new car, with many products and manufacturers, customers need to have several contact points to increase the likelihood of purchase.

Per definition, though, customers stumble by chance across a certain product with accidental marketing. This just by itself is a bad prerequisite for the customer to try and find more contact points with said product. It might always start at the first contact point, which is rarely decisive for the purchase – as tedious as it is unsuccessful.

According to the customer journey idea, customers are more likely to buy products, for instance, that are in the same environment as the products that they had just bought or were interested in before. For instance, they are more likely to buy tools in a DIY store. The customer journey should take place in a certain thematically uniform space.

A pair of work gloves at the till in the DIY store fulfills this requirement and are therefore placed in situational marketing – they are part of the same theme as the wooden boards for interior fitting which customers are pushing toward the till, plus, work gloves protect against splinters while loading the boards into the car.

It works similarly with chocolate bars in the petrol station since they may give the driver new energy for the next leg of the journey.

Products will have a harder time being sold when they break with the theme of other made purchases or do not fit the sales location or the salesperson. Therefore, only one conclusion can be drawn from the reflections on this marketing stage: avoid accidental marketing as much as possible.

If, for instance, the product needs to be sold at a higher price or product benefits are not absolutely clear to the customer, only very special features of the product can lead to an impulse purchase. However, these are rarely in the supplier's interest: extremely low prices, phenomenal discounts or an elaborate sales process with explanatory TV stations like in the DIY store, which must immediately follow the accidental situation.

Level 3: Brand trust marketing

According to Seth Godin, the third level of marketing is based on the brand itself.

Regarding visibility, this level is especially interesting since history and authority are accentuated more against relevance, yet, marketing still works better here than on the previous two levels.

As we have seen earlier with spam marketing, only highly unlikely content relevance can trigger impulse purchases. In the case of random marketing, fortunate circumstances can certainly add relevance in terms of time and content. Relevance is less necessary in marketing with brands because the customer makes their purchase decision for other reasons: they trust a brand.

An example of such visibility could be a customer who stops at the dealership or store of their favorite car brand. There is an increasingly developing form of car experience, especially with luxury brands, which is set up like an app store, presenting cars more as a "brand experience." It is even unnecessary for customers to have bought a car here and are now interested in other products.

Maybe the car dealer offers them some winter tires on aluminium rims. Customers know that other suppliers, such as secondary suppliers, also sell those, and that they tend to be cheaper than the manufacturer's. Still, customers are happy to accept just the manufacturer's guidance function. The trusted manufacturer will certainly have tested the winter tires and rims well, and they will fit the vehicle model just as well. This then saves customers research effort and time. With brands which are particularly connected to a certain reputation, it is also considered appropriate to drive up on brand rims and perhaps use higher-priced sports tires.

Buyers also like to show off their optimized tires during their weekly shopping – mind you, tires with which they could drive their Porsche in the reference lap on the Nürburgring with 1.5 seconds less than with nonoptimized tires. Interestingly, with brands, customers tend to pay more attention to promises than to real benefits.

This last fact becomes even more clear when the manufacturer suddenly offers customers products which have, in actuality, nothing much to do with the theme at hand, for instance sun glasses or holdalls. Granted, a holdall that optimally fits the boot of a Porsche 911 would still fit the theme. And so do sun glasses while traveling into the sunset in a convertible. Yet, the value of a Porsche biro or an Audi espresso maker is *only* fueled by the car brand itself.

The content's and temporal relevance are of secondary importance because these customers do not look primarily for product benefits – instead they are after brand benefits.

Many customers may still be aware of the fact that Porsche, with its own sub-brand "Porsche Design," licenses its design expertise, which is inextricably linked to the brand, to other manufacturers who can then buy a reputable and thought-out design. In this case, it is good when Porsche designs other products for everyday life, still, customers pay extra for the brand imprint.

Is Audi particularly good at building espresso machines? Technical quality distinguishes the brand's cars, but does this extend to all product areas? This is primarily about the brand, which enters into a strange relationship with the product benefit. Apparently, customers buy the brand benefit, but they seem to want to use the brand label more than the product itself, thus, deriving an abstract benefit from it.

As long as the brand cannot or should not play a major role, the product benefit seems quite clear: a product's benefit is directly linked to its function. A pair of no-name shoes protects the wearer's feet and, depending on its functional design, can be worn during sports, a hike or a theater premiere. At most, this product benefit has a weak connection to the company brand that manufactures this product – at least as long as these are not shoes of a popular brand.

No-name products or discounter value brands show a low charge with higher attributes: products being sold by supermarket chains in different product lines mostly have the primary feature of being cheap. The supermarket value brands support the essential core value of low prices right down to the product design (their packaging might be just plain and white) and even down to the naming: "Just Essentials" (previously, "Smart Price") at Asda, for instance. Here, the brand name simply underlines that they sell only the most important food to the "essential" (or "smart") price. Yet, no one buys a carton of milk from "Just Essentials" in order to get some of the brand's shine with it.

Products with weak brands clearly elevate the price to the most important differentiator in the fight for customer favor – the brand becomes more of a low-price indicator.

With supposedly high-quality brands like Mercedes Benz or Louis Vuitton, the connections are very different.

If a brand is positioned more strongly in this game, it first begins to "charge" itself from the most diverse sources. This could be famous brand faces shown in advertising. Great brand visibility could be established at sporting events, for instance. Brands could also be charged by the attribution of special quality, such as Swiss pocket knives from Victorinox or particularly high-quality wristwatches from Jaeger-LeCoultre.

The product attributes, closely tied to its function, are suddenly joined by secondary attributes. People can use the same product as famous personalities, thus, basking in their glamour, well, at least tell themselves that they do. The celebrity is just turned into a projection surface. Or the product's primary attributes, like high precision or high-quality workmanship, prove – as a secondary product attribute and benefit – the customer to be a technology lover, wealthy person or connoisseur of these special aspects.

However, this concept of a brand could (nearly) never be established without a story. This brings the third large element of smart visibility forcefully to the fore. Brand marketing has usually a lot to do with authority and storytelling, having less relevance in most individual cases – at least, regarding the primary product use.

Breitling watches, for instance, tell a number of stories that are essentially tied to the manufacturer's brand. To begin with, they are produced in Switzerland, which is considered an excellent production location for fine mechanical instruments and carries traditional values such as security, prosperity and a certain cosmopolitan mindset. Quite a few Swiss watchmakers are generally regarded as symbols of a certain prosperity because they get paid handsomely for their (often handmade) products. Other stories that tie in with the brand are, for instance, famous actors being repeatedly featured in adverts.

Also because of its own history, in which particularly pilots preferred Breitling watches for various reasons, the brand claims to be a "pilot's brand." It is a running gag amongst today's Breitling buyers that nearly no one can explicate the speed of an aircraft or something else with the style-defining slide rule bezel of the Navitimer model, which clearly references aviation history and allows numerous aviation calculations. Originally, that was the product's main use, but now the product benefit is completely subordinate to the "brand benefit."

Pilots and actors bring their own attributes to all of this, which in a clever marketing-driven interplay bring about a positive brand recognition and a charging of its brand with many positive associations.

All of this often has little to do with the product's actual usefulness, even to the point of nearly grotesque dimensions as with the Breitling Navitimer. For instance, a watch that costs 10 euros and is equipped with a quartz mechanism and battery can also tell the time – as can a 10,000 euro Breitling with a manufacture stature, a winding driven by arm movements and a bearing of the moving parts with dozens of small jewels. It is funny considering that the cheap watch does what we would see as the watch's product benefit – mostly even with more precision than the Swiss manufacture watches are capable of. With the latter, a deviation of only a few seconds a day can already be considered highly precise timekeeping – due to the high-quality mechanical construction. Yet, quartz watch mechanisms provide this product benefit – of measuring the time – far more precisely.

Still, customers appreciate such a product primarily for its brand benefit. The brand ties in all the positive qualities, such as the use by celebrities, fancy technical sophistication or the special brand history, the high price and prestige, all of which make these qualities visible. For many people, a luxury watch, a pair of branded trainers or an expensive handbag, for instance, are legible, they connote all the aforementioned positive qualities that are clearly more strongly linked to the brand than to the actual product.

Customers appreciate that the brand makes these values visible. A luxury watch proves the wearer to be able to invest the purchase price.

A pair of trainers can also make certain qualities visible for its wearers. Among young people, the shoes could be read as a status symbol and one of belonging to certain subcultures, while the same pair of trainers could distinguish a suit-wearer as a progressive, youthful and dynamic doer who just slightly breaks with the usual etiquette. However, the facts that a management consultant does not necessarily have to wear sneakers and that they are probably manufactured under the same production conditions as the cheap no-name sports shoes take a back seat to the brand's glamour.

It is inconceivable to make a brand without considering the factors of time and long-lasting visibility. Traditions, successes and simply the brand experience as well as its visibility in the most diverse contexts charge its very characteristics, thus, ultimately the brand itself over time. These can become secondary product attributes for everything the brand has to offer.

> Brands are mostly made of stories and long-lasting visibility – both of which need time to develop.

And yet, brand trust marketing is not the highest level of marketing, even though it already has many very desirable characteristics with its added relevance, authority and even stories. These factors can reinforce marketing, just as one of them can become so strong that it outshines everything else.

It may well be that brand trust marketing is the highest level for certain companies – and that is not bad at all! It may be impossible to go beyond this level due to the specific market situation or company structure – this may not even be detrimental, it just marks a natural limit to visibility. This form of marketing has its own power and could already make all the difference, depending on the market situation.

Level 4: Personal relationship marketing

On the fourth level of marketing, the three forces of smart visibility grow together even further. The connection between relevance (both regarding time and content), storytelling and authority intensifies and forms a strong basis of smart visibility.

This also makes it clear that personal relationship marketing is actually an augmentation of brand trust marketing – both share many characteristics and criteria. Moreover, trust and a customer relationship are usually formed from a brand that has been cultivated particularly well and over a long time.

It is a good thing when customers have known the Nivea brand for a long while, but it is better if they trust it. Which they do because they use it themselves and have made good experiences with it, and because their grandmother has also always used it.

For personal relationship marketing, authority is the first and foremost factor and is strengthened with the brand. This puts this sort of marketing onto the next level, level 4. It is closely connected to the authority of the people or company. Authority, on the other hand, is based on different aspects of a person or a company, from which it also draws its strength.

This might be, for one thing, the setting in which you meet them, for instance in regards to their certificates or trainings, and in the function in which they meet you. It might even be the company's fame or reputation, having made a name for itself as a high-quality brand.

An example of a person's authority: you would probably attribute more authority to your treating cardiologist while they examine your heart inside their clinic, than when they explain a referee's decision to you in the football stadium without being asked. You would probably take their diagnoses rather seriously in lieu of their expertise, since the examination takes place in their practice and due to their function – perhaps less so in football. You would, on the other hand, more likely accept an analysis of a team's performance from a professional football coach, but you would obviously not let them cut your chest open.

Authority gives these people, companies or brands a power of interpretation. If a renowned brand has a product on offer, then this brand can even partly determine which aspect has relevance in this area and which does not. Customers often trust this interpretation quickly and reliably, boosting visibility.

So, authority is the absolutely decisive factor for relationship marketing based on trust. However, the other two factors of smart visibility also play a large part.

Relevance as a basis for decision-making also emerges quite clearly in relationship marketing. Customers want trust especially for products that are highly relevant to them. However, the offer as such also plays a role. When buying a coffee to go at the train station while passing through, customers will place less emphasis on trust and will not first put the sellers through their paces – they may, however, seek out a bakery chain whose brand they trust. Whereas trust plays a much larger role when choosing a pram or a family doctor.

The question of the importance of trust depends on many criteria, such as relevance, price, the product's influence on the customer's life and the duration of use, purchase frequency and more. With personal relationship marketing, companies and suppliers can sell products with particularly high relevance really well, are normally scrutinized suspiciously and have a great influence on customers – often, these are truly lucrative.

As was just pointed out, companies who are trusted and seen as an authority by customers interpret to a certain extent what has any relevance at all. Therefore, these two pillars of smart visibility are strongly pronounced on this level of marketing and depend on each other. Products for which customers need to have trust are usually products or services intended to solve relatively large problems for said customers, i.e. they are particularly relevant.

Impulse purchases, on the other hand, are an opposite pole to such products with a high demand on trust. Products that can be successfully promoted with trust very rarely get sold on an impulse. Still, personal relationship marketing can very well ensure that customers decide on a product quickly but much smarter than with impulse buying.

Take a mechanic at a car repair shop, for instance. If they recommend a high-quality engine oil for your car, this is a great influence on your decision as a customer. The trusted mechanic inherits authority from the brand they represent. After all, that brand, i.e. the shop, has trained the mechanic to take the best care of and make the best repair and maintenance decisions for cars there.

Ideally, if customers ask the foreman about a purchase decision (the title itself is another insignia of their authority), whom they have known for a long time, then there is a high probability that customers will follow the given recommendation.

Again, the temporal factor plays an important role here, namely in the form of stories that connect both people and also charge the brand with trust. The customer knows the mechanic well and has gained positive experiences with them. Their skill and authority have shown themselves in the previous customer relationship. An authority can establish itself in the overlap of good stories, the setting of the brand workshop and the mechanic's position as foreman – and certainly not least on the basis of the mechanic's competent, ever decent personality.

Customers then find little reason for doubt when deciding on an expensive premium motor oil. At that very moment, there is little opportunity for any other orientation on product characteristics and comparable products, thus, trusting blindly. This trust, which promises orientation, is tied to the person of the workshop foreman, but it can be replaced by the knowledgeable neighbor or the report in an automobile magazine.

People like to trust people because they rely on their own competence of classification of others. The basic trust of being able to trust one's fellow human beings, at least to a certain extent, is what only makes societies with shared work, tasks and power possible, and is deeply rooted.

Therefore, the three factors of smart visibility are very well represented in the fourth marketing level. This might now make you wonder why an overlap of relevance, authority and storytelling, which together yield the best results in visibility, does not mean the highest level of marketing.

This is, on the one hand, due to weighting. There is certainly still room for improvement regarding the relevance that customers bring to personal relationship marketing. However, problems do exist that are so urgent that an excess of relevance on the customer's side actually reduces the importance of authority and, above all, storytelling – while still allowing for a higher level of marketing. What may sound counter-intuitive at first in the light of the model of the three factors of smart visibility will resolve itself with the last two levels – please bare with me for a moment.

Even the topics of authority and stories, which are both so immensely important for visibility, can become more apparent than with personal relationship marketing. Whenever customers take on responsibility and try to get an image as objectively as possible of product attributes, this is an assault on the brand and the trust in sellers, consultants and other authorities.

For instance, the workshop foreman will face the justified suspicion that they only recommended a certain engine oil that allows for a better margin. Of course, in their role, they are not completely unbiased. This limits their maximum amount of authority as a point of orientation for customers and their trust.

Still, when companies succeed in establishing their own brand with marketing – it does not really matter whether they are individual suppliers or large companies – then this is a high level of marketing that has a chance of success: a level of marketing that is superior to that of many competitors.

Therefore, it is a lofty goal to be a good brand with controlled relevance, storytelling and authority, in which customers put their trust. When a company manages this, it has done a lot correctly.

Ultimately, the following two levels of visibility are special cases of the fourth level of visibility. Certain factors stand out particularly well here, or the market's accompanying factors or the customer's problems are special. However, these levels are interesting starting points for fine-tuning your own visibility.

Level 5: Loyalty marketing

The fifth level describes the close relationship between customers and a provider. A good example of this are influencers, as they are very successful in offering their followers such loyalty marketing. When a brand with a strong connection to its customers launches a new product, the products are less scrutinized and questioned, thus, have far fewer marketing obstacles to overcome.

The same is true for a YouTube channel with trusting followers and fans, or if customers identify very strongly with a brand for other reasons. Sometimes marketing is no longer perceived as advertising – at least at this level it loses many of the negative associations that customers have with marketing. This is why loyalty marketing can be classified as very successful.

If there is a strong bond with a brand, customers often stop questioning the products which they usually would if they were afraid of making a mistake. Customers also no longer experience the messages of advertising as an attempt to be wooed or even persuaded: since they already have been and are.

Perhaps they instead experience this content as a welcome offer of information and for orientation. They experience the products and companies as privileged access to solutions to their most pressing problems. They also have a deep-seated trust in the brand and its offers and that the latter would satisfy their needs on different levels. This may be especially true for secondary attributes which are normally hard to fathom and to put into words in marketing for advertisers.

Best case, the purchase of a brand becomes its own value: buying a Gucci handbag might turn the buying process itself into an upscale happening.

Exciting interactions happen when there are close bonds to a brand or such disseminators, especially at the overlap between a customer's need for guidance and the company's orientation offers or the disseminator's information and advertising offers. This close bond has a very positive effect: the authority of the companies and people to whom the customers bind themselves motivates them to trust the offers and follow them. To put it more bluntly: the closer and more trusting the bond, the easier it is for customers to follow recommendations.

If a good bond can be established to this extend, then customers will voluntarily accept the company's guidance function. After all, it meets a distinct guidance need. In sum, this is a win-win situation for both customers and companies – at least, as long as companies make really good offers for customers, while the customers are looking for the companies' products.

Every company concerned about or wanting to improve the visibility of its offers should check these highest levels of marketing.

This is especially true for brands relying on high levels of customer loyalty, they can increase their authority over customers to such an extent that both product attributes and customers' traditional evaluation criteria are viewed separately. If a brand with immense customer connections or if a successful influencer as an intermediary presents products to their followers, then it is certainly common for them to consider the offered information and purchase possibility as being relevant without having to be checked.

The same can be observed at the highest levels of marketing for companies; they can sell products to their fans partly unchecked. We have all seen pictures of people queuing in front of Apple stores for a new device that is about to be launched.

Apple products, for instance, cannot only do marketing with their own brand, which, as was described above, revolves primarily around secondary product attributes (i.e. those that have little or no connection to the product function), but these are enhanced to such an extent that the competition would hardly be able to dissuade them from their brand loyalty.

> It is almost impossible to persuade an Apple iPhone user to switch to Xiaomi or Samsung, for instance. Apple has built a fence made of extremely strong customer loyalty and its own ecosystem around its customers. Even if a customer intends to leave the Apple product sphere, this would result in downstream problems: what happens to App store purchases? How can photos or contacts be transferred?

Particularly this example shows that the product's performance parameters as well as the price-performance ratio and the relations to technical equipment of competing products become less important. Apple should actually fear its competition – measured purely in terms of parameters, price-performance ratio and technological ability.

In its strongest manifestation, authority can take on a guidance function that can affect the other factors. It simply determines what is relevant for followers – or for brand disciples. Then, this construct endures even if the stories are weak. It is important that the story's heroes are especially strong – for instance, the highly revered influencer or the admired singer with an Instagram account or the strong Apple brand.

In many ways, Instagram accounts are also channels for storytelling, even if the plot (heroes, turning points, challenges, etc.) often falls flat. Yet, a camper on a little adventure in every video, who tests products that make his life easier, also tells a bonding tale. Still, his authority, the authentic way he tells his story, his impartiality because he is *not* a manufacturer, and the way his videos are made (which do not have to be of cinema quality) allow him to create a close bond with his viewers, who then buy into his narrative and him as being unquestionably credible. This is the main reason why large (as well as small and medium-sized) companies increasingly refrain from creating elaborately produced scatter marketing, instead increasingly seek help from influencers. If this form of marketing is cheaper, simpler and also more successful, there is not really much to think about.

Companies have also developed the most diverse and sometimes remarkable concepts to create personal relationships with their customers: for instance, Ferrari customers can only buy some models if they have previously taken part in events organized by the brand, have already bought other models from them and who have proven themselves (by way of personal contact) to be good brand ambassadors. Anyone wanting to buy a special Ferrari – maybe because other community members can then read this as a sign and because it is so rare – must make a strong commitment to the brand. It is not enough anymore to just pay the purchase price. The local Ford dealer will certainly be less strict in this regard when you want to buy a car there.

This is an extraordinary form of marketing: to have customers formally ask to be allocated a product by strongly binding them to said product. Yet, it works when the product is exceptional and can solve some of the customer needs well because the brand and products have a special visibility and can shine their light onto customers.

Level 6: Intravenous marketing

According to Seth Godin's model, intravenous marketing is the highest form of marketing refinement. It can hardly be explained without its most significant example, which also gave it its name, after all.

In this story, a patient with a life-threatening heart attack enters a hospital's emergency room. The patient is hoping for help. This turns them into one of the hospital's and the treating doctor's customers, thus, is visible to the hospital.

The doctor suggests the patient be given an infusion and that medicine be administered; obviously, the patient agrees and gets the IV. Afterwards, the doctor directs all the clinic's products and offers deemed medically necessary directly to the patient, without asking for permission again. The patient is of good faith and relies on the doctor to do the right thing.

The patient will most certainly not question the situation or compare it with other offers. They will hardly refuse treatment and instead demand: "Please drive me to another hospital, I would like to compare their offers for life-saving measures with the ones here – both regarding prices and content."

The offer's relevance stands above all and is pronounced to the maximum. The customer's life is at stake – there is nothing that could be more relevant. This relevance also has a strong temporal component since the solution is urgent. Thus, it is so strong that authority and stories take a back seat. Even if doubt about their competence arose due to the behavior of the attending physician during the placement of the venous access – relevance and the hope for the problem solution would outshine this doubt about authority by *a lot*.

Moreover, the stories the doctor could use in marketing his treatment are probably also manageable. At this point, for both doctor and patient, it is primarily a matter of exceeding relevance.

This type of marketing would show itself to be weaker than, for instance, personal relationship marketing when measured against the three dimensions of smart visibility. Yet, this is only the partial truth.

First of all, intravenous marketing is Godin's highest form of marketing for other reasons. After all, in his metaphor, the customer stops to check any of the supplier's product offerings, instead, giving them carte blanche to deliver any and all products to them – in the deepest confidence and belief that they are of greatest relevance to them.

A look at actual marketing examples shows that this is neither a rare occurrence nor does it necessarily presuppose life-threatening conditions.

So imagine, for instance, a product being offered to you on the Internet: you are supposed to buy an app that would solve a problem for you, it might improve your golf game like the app "Hole 19." For one month, you would be able to use it free of charge (this is the permission to put the cannula of the infusion into you); after that the provider charges a monthly subscription fee (until you cancel).

Whole industries are based on this model: Spotify, for instance, or Netflix or the football subscription on Sky. Many of such products are very successful on the Internet, and most of them work as subscriptions. Even outside of the digital contexts, subscriptions are a model of customer loyalty that has long been tried, tested and loved by companies.

Customers give their consent once here as well to receive this provider's future products. Be it digital or physical – customers order a subscription once, to be from then on exposed to these offers.

Customers might become "Amazon Prime" members and from then on willingly use the advantages of their subscriptions, such as access to media, preferential parcel deliveries – from which Amazon earns money – and also willingly offer comprehensive information on their usage and purchase behavior, which the company can then use for a profit.

This type of connection between customers and Amazon has clear features of intravenous marketing and is cleverly constructed. Customers once give their consent to a membership and enjoy a number of benefits. All these benefits are structured in such a way that the company always also benefits from the respective interaction between customers and company. It is both a give and certainly a take for the company.

The aforementioned subscription models for info products also know such intravenous follow-up deals. Upselling is one such example.

In marketing, it is assumed that higher-priced products have poorer chances at the first or second contact points with customers. It takes a lot of the provider's energy to sell a high-priced product at such an early stage of customer contact.

With digital marketing, in particular, however, many providers shy away from such high-energy services because they involve personnel costs and are expensive. Instead, they take a different approach and first offer the customer a low-priced product that represents an impulse purchase like a single symbolic euro. This is a basic offer, but it meets high expectations. Customers, faced with this fantastic offer, are now ready to forget their doubts: the impulse becomes too strong. Suddenly it seems like a mistake not to buy the product.

This initial deal probably works because it has little to no risk. It is either a cheap purchase or an incredible offer. Directly after the purchase, customers are made another offer, for instance, a premium membership like on XING[3]. With this, they already unconsciously associate the provider with various positive qualities, including authority and storytelling.

Customers are suddenly their own testimonials because they have bought something from the provider and have now received a substantial but low-priced offer. Moreover, they already know the provider, maybe even have already created their profile on XING.

In this way, you can use the marketing advantages of intravenous marketing for your own company. It is explicitly a fair deal for both sides: customers get a lot for their initial impulse purchase, after all, it is meant to be attractive to them.

In regards to its morality, this business model is evaluated afterwards as of whether the infusion is abused in the process. This is somewhat more pronounced in old media, in daily newspapers, than in digital contexts: customers are put on the infusion with a 14-day trial subscription to a daily newspaper. And before they know it, they are stuck with it until its long cancelation period expires.

Still, intravenous marketing is also a good illustration of how to work with customers when a company knows their expectations well, when it solves their problems frequently and reliably really well, when the cooperation benefits both and a deep relationship of trust ensues.

However, the biggest advantage is an ongoing revenue stream from recurring subscription payments.

Peloton: an example of an intravenous product universe

Peloton has integrated many features of intravenous visibility really well into its own business model. Accordingly, the brand has become successful in a very short time and has secured high visibility and large sales in the market: the number of global customers has increased by a total of 113 percent from 2019 to 2020; at the beginning of 2020, Peloton had as much as 1.1 million customers.[4]

The company is now estimated to be worth over 8 billion euros.

The Peloton brand offers indoor fitness bikes and treadmills. This in and of itself is an old hat since "ergometers" moved into the living rooms and studies during the economic boom in the 1950s. So the business model's core is anything but new.

Peloton bikes are equipped with large displays that show online courses and are connected to the Internet. This is more than just adding to the possibilities of digitization: it has reinvented this business model and the visibility of the product itself.

On demand or live, exercising customers are connected via the bike with actual trainers and training groups of other digitally connected customers. So while everyone's sitting on their home fitness bike, they can see a trainer. The latter is used for the coordination of the warm-up training on the bike, then the difficulty level is increased, with different intensities interspersed throughout the training.

Still, even that is not too spectacular; ultimately, a DVD or a good reference book with a training plan and a stopwatch could do. Peloton, however, rethinks customer loyalty further to intravenous visibility.

The (mostly female) trainers address the whole group directly and personally. Pace changes are announced, and there is a general motivational address. This alone speaks to psychological patterns, creating a bond between customer and offer. The group dynamic motivates people to join a class with their familiar training group on Thursday mornings, for instance. Though participants do not see each other, the group dynamic still functions similarly to analog contexts – with the trainers making sure of it. If a group event is offered on a regular basis, then it takes more effort to stay away than perhaps the actual effort of doing the sports. If nothing else, this is the magic of gym appointments or running groups.

The coaches do not see the home athletes either – but they do see their performance data. Those who show a slower performance than others or than their previous performances stand out and can be addressed directly by name. To some, this may sound like a description of one of George Orwell's dystopian novels, but it is the necessary transparency of motivation that customers are looking for, including the possibility of training correction and encouragement.

Thus, customers can outsource the problem of sports motivation and buy themselves free of this burden with a subscription of 39 pounds. This is a directly implemented customer benefit and intravenous marketing. The fact that customers do not have to transmit their data, can only perceive the other participants through the intermediary Peloton (participants can make their data visible to each other) and can also simply leave the device switched off seems to be just the right degree of freedom and control.

However, customers leave behind user anonymity and become visible to the company. This is basically the logic of a gym class, where the trainers get to know their course participants with time, can observe their individual performance developments and motivate them further. This part was transferred to the digital world because it works well offline.

Trainers are notably visible, since you can check out the trainer profiles on the Peloton website. These are often detailed, the person is meant to be recognizable and customers are meant to feel like they are training with people they know rather well.

Besides the question of whether these descriptions are accurate and honest, clients can get to know their trainers and make their own choices. Trainers also upload personal music lists, which are then played for all course participants during the session for further motivation and were also personally selected by the trainer for their group.

So Peloton not only bonds customers to its products but also offers them brand representatives for a personal connection. Maybe people are less likely to give up ties to other people than they are to a disdainful product – even if it costs a good 2,000 pounds.

For the idea of smart visibility, this form of mutual visibility is sensational: while using the product, the customer suddenly becomes visible to the company. And the company – visible through the trainer – not only motivates them to continue working on their own goals but also to use the product. While it can control this usage. This is especially interesting because the course usage happens as a subscription, so Peloton not only collects money with the expensive bikes but also generates automatic other payments.

For over 2,000 pounds, customers only get the Peloton bike, also available in two versions: in the higher-priced version, for instance, the trainer adjusts the level of exertion, while customers have to turn the wheel themselves with the cheaper version.

The courses, though, must always be purchased and paid for on a monthly basis. After a cancelation of the subscription, the display remains black, at least as far as the courses and external monitoring of achieved goals are concerned. This also means that the Peloton loses its unique selling point compared to normal ergometers. There is no trainer motivation any longer, which also applies to the regularity of the training groups and the sense of community. By canceling their subscription, customers would give up an essential aspect of the purchase.

Which they know very well. People want to have the best of both worlds with the Peloton bike: on the one hand, they might not want to have to go to the gym, reasons being manifold. On the other hand, they do not want to miss out on the motivational power of courses with trainers and other participants. Maybe they want to integrate the courses better into their daily lives, while avoiding the disadvantages of a gym infrastructure. Maybe they still want to be motivated and need an extra stimulus for their sessions.

So in total, customers buy the high-priced ergometer and then still pay monthly course fees. On top of that, additional weights, fitted shoes and other gimmicks can be added to the attractively priced package purchases.

Peloton has obviously really understood and internalized the marketing phrase "The best buyer is the buyer," and has put it to use. After all, what could be a greater sign of trust by customers than buying the higher-priced product on offer? At this level, further offers are easily made. The company has a high visibility toward its customers, while customers are very interested – which they have proven.

The solution relevance was conveyed in an understandable manner and the customers' sufficiently pressing problem was addressed. Doing further business with such customers is highly attractive for Peloton, thus, a form of smart visibility. Customers in such models are usually very willing to purchase even more products.

If everything goes according to plan, service providers know such customer relations. They provide a service for their customers and they in turn are satisfied with it. If the other parameters of these business conditions also fit, like price, execution and speed, for instance, then it is very likely that customers will book something else – as long as a continuous problem is being involved.

Marketing or services for home or garden are two examples from very different areas that can be turned into years of continuous customer relation. They have the search for convenience and orientation in common, and customers are usually satisfied with a solution for a long while, once it is found. Then, they are happy to accept further services of this kind.

Still, it is worth taking a look at how "Peloton-like," intravenous, that is, your own customer model is. It is not limited to service providers: when creating websites or digital client offers, for instance, agencies could always consider attaching a maintenance contract. This can be a win-win situation, in which clients pass on later maintenance and security costs of their website to the agency, thus solving a future problem.

Yet, manufacturers of physical products can also think in terms of such product universes. Ideally, the process is not completed by the product purchase but only started in a highly qualified manner. Just by thinking this way, a business model can be changed from a marketing that is continuously trying to gain visibility to a comfortable marketing with smart visibility toward motivated and good customers.

Gamification for customer loyalty

One final thought about Peloton that could also be instructive for your marketing. They use elements of gamification for their customer retention – the continued visibility of product benefits to customers. Computer games or even board games know aspects that we have mentioned regarding storytelling, which always fascinate and often motivate people: a clearly defined goal and certain challenges along the way. Playfully, customers measure themselves against these and ambitiously pursue the goals.

As a rule, to win a game, there are certain parameters within which the goal must be achieved. With board games like *Ludo*, the goal is to be the first to move all pieces to certain squares – assuming some luck with the dice and a sound strategy. Platform computer games are mostly about mastering a certain course and challenge within a certain time frame. It is always the goal to achieve a certain performance, either beat the time, the competition or your own result last time.

For this very reason, Peloton has an app that tracks the performance of its customers very precisely and makes it transparent to customers – by the way, if desired, also to trainers and other group members. On the one hand, customers can see their own progress and show it to others; on the other hand, they can see how they are gradually reaching their goals. This is a continuous motivation because small milestones seem to be within reach rather than the bigger picture – especially since their own fitness goals are self-set and flexible, i.e. they can also be changed.

Managing "10 kilometers on the Peloton bike in under 20 minutes" or being "the best in the group": when the goal is too far away it loses its luster. Small goals are easier to reach and keep customers motivated.

This way, Peloton can prove in small increments that the investment of the monthly subscription is worth the money – after all, they were now one or two minutes faster or are now fitter than before.

Quite intelligently, Peloton motivates its customers with gamification to further walk along the highest form of visibility, and manages to build their next component for intravenous visibility.

Different steps of visibility need different levels of consent by customers

Following the six levels of Seth Godin's model and from a company's perspective, the visibility value increases with every level. This in itself is a great added value in the pursuit of smart visibility – in contrast to messages that are interchangeable and have a worthless visibility.

In order to understand the meaning of the six levels and to be able to optimally use the structure behind them for your own method map for smart visibility, it is very helpful to focus on one single question that connects all marketing level, against which all of the levels must be measured.

This question concerns customers' consent for receiving any marketing and for granting companies any visibility.

These six levels of consent can be classified as follows:

1. Spam has no customer consent.
2. Accidental marketing is unsolicited, but still accepted by customers.
3. Brands are interesting because they have a brand benefit and authority. Therefore, they and their marketing are allowed to be visible to customers.
4. Personal relationship marketing can rely on customers' assumptions that these offers justify their trust and is almost always welcome; customers also actively seek sources for trustworthy product recommendations.
5. Loyalty marketing goes beyond simply allowing visibility; instead, customers now seek it of their own accord.
6. With intravenous marketing, customers give permission once and then allow the company extensive freedom in trying to sell the product.

The axis of development of permission for visibility goes from "unconsented" to "absolute taken-for-grantedness" in which manufacturers are allowed to be regularly visible to customers, selling products to them for this exact purpose.

These are great arguments for developing and improving one's own visibility based on these levels. After all, as customers' consent to visibility increases as much as the desire to do business with this company or supplier, the cost of customer acquisition automatically decreases.

In the long run, it is far more lucrative for a company to make the effort once, achieving higher visibility levels toward its target group and making them permanent fans. On the other hand, it is also good business sense to ask your customers for permission for visibility.

Taking a long view, it is time-consuming, expensive and not very promising to even overcome potential customers' attention threshold with high budgets in scatter marketing, with interchangeable products and shares of spam or random marketing. At the same time, it is every company's dream come true when they can finally get rid of their flyers and business cards because their own loyal and favorite customers recommend the company, or because customers ask on their own volition for new offers or new products, or they might even take out a subscription.

Directed visibility equals turnover

Customers buy the product that solves their problem. For this to happen, they need to understand it and think it to be the best possible deal. In an ideal world, the product has to reach smart visibility for this, it has to stand for a clear solution and be better than other products or options – even a 'nonsale' counts. Only the closing of a deal turns smart visibility into turnover.

A deal as the basis for business

If the company achieves a sufficient overlap between its product and customer needs, a deal is made and only then can turnover be generated.

How exactly does such a deal work? Basically, it works like a balance scale, as held by fictitious Justitia to establish justice.

Intuitively, customers know that a deal needs them to put something on the scale. When companies approach them through visibility, they are supposed to bring attention to the game. Yet, since they expect something in return, companies now successfully use content marketing, for instance, with added valuable information to make the deal look balanced for customers.

Customers, if they are supposed to buy a product, have to put money on the line – so in return they want a deal that is as good as possible. They expect something in return for the two scarce goods – attention and money. The scale must tip in their favor; by the way, "relevance" comes from the Latin word "relevare" – "to bring into balance."

Companies bring in product benefits and advantages to make the offer relevant for customers. These benefits should then be so great that customers regard them as beneficial and, at best, see themselves in the advantage. Fairness often becomes secondary when it is in the customer's favor.

This is known as good value for money or a "bargain."

Additionally, companies can also add so-called "incentives," like gifts, discounts or soft factors, to further entice the purchase. These factors can be a personal relationship with the company or the provider, a certain status exuded by the product, or the idea of doing good. The deal just has to be good, the scales have to be amply filled on the customer's side.

Most of the time, it is difficult for a company to convey all these elements of a good deal to the customer on the first contact. Thus, customers often need several contact points to get an overview of the deal and decide on accepting it.

The rule of seven contact points

Therefore, customers must see an offer more than once; on average, a company needs seven contact points to generate sales from good visibility. Yet, it does not necessarily take all seven – the actual number depends on various factors. While the three pillars of smart visibility influence the number of these factors: relevance, authority and the stories told by a company. They shorten the path between visibility and deal.

If, as with intravenous visibility, an issue is especially relevant, then it will probably need fewer contact points. It also takes fewer contact points when the company has built up quite a bit of authority with its popularity and integrity. And it is also a shortcut when an engaging story mesmerizes the customer during the process of visibility and leads them to a product purchase.

Products with low prices or traditional impulse purchases also need fewer contact points. Yet, products that are very expensive or could have a big impact on the customer's life while not being time-sensitive, on which they would want a lot of information, want to be able to draw comparisons and also want to be as objective as possible, may need a lot of contact points – for instance, a product seen as an investment such as a machine which demands a higher level of consultation.

> Companies need to manage their visibility well and need to own the process of this contact chain. If a company wants to convert its visibility toward its customers into sales, then it must lead them as far away as possible from any accidental decisions. Essentially, managed visibility is the way to go.

Therefore, companies must become visible to their customers in various ways – visibility needs to take place on different channels. It also must be coherent and controlled because when push comes to shove, customers will remember little about the company between individual contact points.

However, for the customer, visibility is condensed from one contact point to another into certain structures, patterns and, probably, stereotypes because customers then start to attribute the company with certain characteristics as well as the product with attributes and problem-solving skills.

So when customers stumble upon a company at one contact point which focuses on cleaning products but offers cough drops at the next, they will hardly be able to condense this into a message. Why should they buy something off this company? This is the reason why the company Procter & Gamble has brands like "Flash" and "Vick" written in large letters on the products instead of the company name.

Furthermore, toxic visibility should be avoided since it can also be condensed to a message; often, incredulity is given more weight by customers than many good arguments. Yet, companies can take customer criticism from certain channels and actively use it for product improvements. Take negative comments on social media, for instance, they need to be taken seriously and turned into (preferably) something positive.

It is also dangerous to assume that channels in which a company does not actively participate would not be important for said company. A prominent example of such a connection is the rating platform Doctify on which doctors are being rated by patients. Some doctors distrust this and consider the rating to be inaccurate, or they simply shy away from being actively involved and putting effort in. However, the consequence of not creating a profile there and not reacting to patient criticism does not mean that doctors are not represented there.

Rather, Doctify creates profiles for every doctor in the country, so that patients can rate them – regardless whether doctors have created their own profiles. This undermines any opportunity to actively counter false criticism or to motivate satisfied patients to leave many good reviews. Thus, "We are not represented on this channel" assumes wrong – instead, unguided, thus, toxic visibility happens.

This example is particularly dangerous since Doctify has a very high Google affinity. Google prefers ratings from actual people to algorithms, mainly because they can beat any form of artificial intelligence in assessing content relevance – well, at least as of yet.

So Google prefers to show Doctify reviews when patients search for a doctor online. So, the first hit on the list of search results might not be the doctor's website but Doctify instead – including its good and bad reviews, which the doctor wanted to keep invisible by ignoring them.

On the same basis, unguided visibility can, for instance, lead hotel portals to punish a hotel for ignoring customer feedback. Here, too, a momentum of its own can develop that can hardly be reeled back in by the company later on.

Cross-channel contacts

The example of Doctify is also appropriate because many doctors do make an effort to gain visibility on Google. Almost all medical practices have a website nowadays. Web agencies are often asked one question by clients wanting a websites: "How will this ensure my visibility on Google?"

Not only doctors think of the following scenario while creating their websites: a potential new client uses Google in the search of a suitable offer. In this case, providers want to be listed above other providers in the struggle for sales. To ensure this, SEO (search engine optimization) is stipulated as an elementary factor of successful marketing when specifying to-dos for the marketing agency booked to build the website.

Instead, it would make far more sense to forego SEO and instead actively outsource this task to rating portals with a link to one's own website.

You can easily control this visibility yourself: after a successful treatment, simply ask your clients or patients openly to rate you and your work on the Internet, emphasizing how much this would help you. A satisfied customer will certainly be happy enough to help you out. This way, you can easily steer your own visibility, also it is free of charge, with a low threshold, yet, a high quality. By asking only satisfied patients for a review, the positive verdicts will stand out all the more in the overall rating.

Still, your own website is a good and central contact point for digitally generated customer attention. A lot of time and effort is invested in determining necessary keywords, which apparently have to be found on the website with the necessary frequency, and in many other criteria. Elaborately produced videos are integrated because developers know that this sort of content is given a preferential treatment by Google and its video portal YouTube. Expensive photos are taken and testimonials are obtained from customers or patients.

And yet, Google usually shows Doctify much more prominently at the top of the list because it beats any individual doctor's website regarding countless parameters that play a role in valuable visibility and Google ranking: Doctify has a lot more content (for instance, data on 30,000 doctors), is clicked on much more frequently by customers (the German equivalent Jameda has more than four million users a month[1]), has thousands of links pointing to further relevant content – all of which are hard SEO factors which the marketing agency otherwise laboriously tries to optimize on the individual doctor's website, thus, failing in comparison with the rating platform.

The energy to motivate already satisfied customers to a good rating is probably less work and cheaper than the booking of an SEO-specialized web agency – and incidentally much more successful because it considers multiple channels. The valuable visibility generated by the rating then leads to the provider's linked website – free of charge. This is how visibility can be used cleverly across channels.

For other professions, there are a number of rating platforms with a similar positive effect: Proven Expert (in the German-speaking area) or Google Reviews for instance. Hotel and travel booking portals also have their own platforms that create visibility.

Indivisible usage must become visible

Information must be managed as well as possible if visibility to customers occurs at different contact points, using different information channels in the process, while visibility can even skip these channels.

Since customers have so many channels to choose from, companies might have a hard time finding a customer's first contact point. Marketing measures that make use of print marketing, such as direct mail or TV spots, increase the likelihood of becoming visible to a customer. Still, at the same time, they have the structural disadvantage of being scatter marketing or might even have to fight the accusation of being spam, which we have discussed several times here.

Customers who seek out their own contact points with the company as well as its associated messages and content are pre-qualified by their own impulse and consider such information as being relevant.

Contact points have to be logical

This makes it all the more important that corporate communication on these channels is coherent. It is of little use to a company if the customer associates it with one problem solution in the first contact and a completely different one in the next. This so-called "indivisible product benefit" must therefore be the focal point of smart visibility.

A customer has to be able to simply and clearly identify and recognize a company at every contact point.

If a company keeps the three pillars of smart visibility in mind, the likelihood that customers will discover relevance, authority and stories offered to them at each contact point is significantly increased.

This automatically attracts customer attention – in a controlled manner. From a first Google search, from a seemingly random contact on Facebook or Instagram, or because a micro-influencer referred to the company or one of its products – customer attention is always drawn to the company and they may be willing to find out more. So companies need to lead the process of their visibility. Successful instruments for directing visibility are, for instance, the so-called Facebook remarketing or an email newsletter. Customers who have shown a general interest in the company contents – which might just be a longer "digital visit" on one of their marketing contents – can be identified very easily by Facebook.

Afterwards, advertisers can run a follow-up ad that slightly deepens the insight into the content of what was just looked at and brings customers closer to the product and the possibility of a deal with more of the same information.

Just as people do not usually ask others to marry them on their first date, companies are also well advised not to immediately confront customers with a sales contract. Customers first want to get more information, and if they cross paths with the company on several contact points thanks to smart visibility, adding a few pieces of information each time, which the customer can then condense into a singular picture, a buying impulse is triggered.

Unfortunately, many providers are unaware of the possibilities at various points of this seven-contact rule and leave too much to chance. This sometimes has to do with the fact that providers believe they cannot do anything at some of the contact points except actually leaving it to chance, instead of just relying on frequency.

One example: someone booked you for a lecture at a symposium. The organizer wants to give you the opportunity to inspire other participants with your best work knowledge, both from employed and self-employed work. While giving the speech, you manage to present your expertise and create a desire amongst potential customers to engage further with you.

Typical speakers now no longer control this generated and good visibility: they assume that potential customers from the auditorium will pave the way for further information themselves. After all, their email address, website and LinkedIn account were on the last Power-

Point slide. Yet, this has become insufficient. After your talk, the audience will try to involve you in a conversation. Unfortunately, this works only briefly in the evening, so that you barely exchange business cards.

However, we all know on some level that business cards are sometimes only found in the jacket weeks later. Thus, smart visibility was not controlled enough. Originally valuable visibility turned into worthless visibility over time.

This is a basic problem of the seven-contact rule: if the problem's relevance is not above average, then the interest momentum between contact points tends to decrease with the passing of time, while other solutions present themselves to the costumers in the meantime.

Even though the topic excited the customer immensely that evening, it will still take a back seat to the day-to-day business in the office the next day.

This means that you first have to find a way to address the customer on your own volition in the future. It makes a huge difference whether the customer can contact you afterwards should the topic still be of interest to them – and they also find the time for it. Or whether you automatically remind the customer of the topic again way shortly after, for instance in a newsletter. Perhaps you could send them a summary of your presentation – just like content marketing, which is aimed at accentuating your offer's most important advantages again, while preparing them for immediate use for their own team. It is then that you remain the owner of your visibility.

The aforementioned newsletter comes in handy here. It makes it clearly visible that you steer your own visibility: with a newsletter and a collection of valuable contacts from various contact points, you are put in a position of actively addressing customers with qualified content, while the competition is still hoping that customers will accidentally stumble upon their website.

To fill the list of your newsletter recipients, it is important to give customers a clear call to action (CTA). A Power Point slide with the information on how to find your website is an insufficient CTA: it does not present the customer with an attractive deal – even though they might be invited to draw their attention to you and your content a second time. Yet, customers are lazy, they see their own need for guidance not being represented here or do not see an advantage in this interaction – thus, such general, flat appeals of making contact seldomly work.

Customers tend to be the opposite of proactive, they do not want to call a place, instead, they put off that important information until the next day, and are usually satisfied enough with the, albeit criticizable, status quo to not expend energy on changing anything. Instead, it works much better, if you give customers a clear, benefit-oriented CTA with a clear goal and a clear offer.

For instance, at the end of the presentation, you could make potential new customers an offer to have the just presented contents conveniently sent to them via email as a PDF. For this, they just need to send you a short email to a specified address, or send you a message via WhatsApp to a specified telephone number – for you to then send them the prepared content. With readily available digital email and contact management systems, you can then collect the contact data and add it to your newsletter address pool. This way, you control your own visibility.

Furthermore, here, both sides win: customers receive high-quality information on a relevant topic and are approached by you again. Since the topic is relevant to them, they even look forward to being contacted by you.

In sum, this creates a so-called funnel, a customer funnel. Easily realized and cheap visibility becomes guided visibility through various tools.

This visibility, carrying a clear and unambiguous message, then increasingly condenses into a customer's purchase interest. This then comes increasingly to a head via switch functions – as, incidentally, does the customer's interest in more information. Each contact is such a switch, at which the customer decides whether you will now follow the customer journey together – or go separate ways.

Inside the funnel, the first contact points tend to be characterized by high-quality information. With later contact points, more sales momentum is added each time. It is only here that your customer should contact you or buy your product. Then, it is basically about giving them the necessary information and contact points that will help them with the purchase decision.

> Only a systematically built funnel will turn your visibility into controlled visibility and your potential customer into an actual one.

Visibility on social media is twice as expensive

Do you actually "own" your followers? Most companies do not even ask themselves this question, even though platforms like Facebook, Instagram, YouTube and LinkedIn can close your account and basically without batting an eye.

Actually, that is something that Facebook does, and quite regularly, I might add. The company Facebook does not disclose numbers on how many company or marketing accounts it suspends. Articles on unblocking pages and advertising accounts, on legal help and also on editorial content from computer online periodicals can be found ten a penny.

If a company or a user posts content or creates advertising, Facebook will check it. Mere inorganic content is treated somewhat more leniently than paid content. Facebook checks the latter intensively and only explicitly releases it after checking for content violations against standards set up and applied by Facebook.

Overall, organic content is treated more liberally because it is assumed that there is no explicit economic interest at heart, which users would complain about to Facebook as being misleading.

Consequently, organic and inorganic content are different. When organic content does not comply with community standards, this usually leads to a temporary block of the account. Advertising that does not meet Facebook's standards is often punished much more severely. Many entrepreneurs and even larger companies can report on being blocked from using Facebook as an advertisement opportunity and, thus, from their many painstakingly assembled followers.

Yet, even if everything is in order, Facebook still reserves itself the right to decide which users can see which organic content posted by a company.

When confronted with criticism about not all followers seeing all the content all the time, the company argues that this would simply be too large an amount of content for users to not be overwhelmed. Which in turn would harm Facebook and the advertising companies. In addition, there are topical limits – when it comes to displaying posts, some topics are given preferential treatment, while others are not. It gets even worse: large accounts organically reach fewer of their followers than accounts with few followers.

Besides content quantity, Facebook also uses relevance as a yardstick: users should only see content that is as relevant as possible. Especially regarding organic content, for which companies do not pay, Facebook filters immensely and only lets a single-digit percentage of the content through to respective users. Since Facebook is the only company to exercise its digital "householder's" rights for content, this process does not always seem fair and transparent.

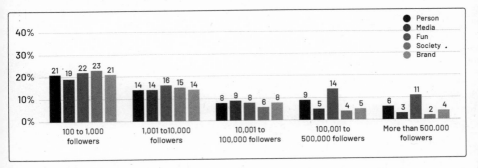

Not all your followers see your posts, far from it. The illustration depicts the average Instagram reach per follower, broken down into sectors. The example proves that only a small fraction of your followers actually get to see your posts. Even worse: the more followers you have, the lesser your reach.

Source: original illustration according to an idea and data from Fanpage Karma[2]

Ignoring the power of interpretating content and the question of whether Facebook is actually able to decide what is truly relevant for a company's followers, this is a process that statistically works against companies who want to organically address their followers: if marketing budget is put forth to gain 1,000 or 10,000 new followers, then this is truly challenging if, of these 1,000 followers, only 7 or 8 percent get to see an organic post afterwards. Leaving the logic of getting the best possible return on marketing budget void.

The basic business logic could still be: we gain followers and can then rely on this safe bank of accessibility for potential customers. Yet, this approach has pretty much stopped working.

However, Facebook itself is offering a solution: you can pay for and place adverts that are then shown to your own target audience. Thus, informing your own followers costs you twice: the first time for them to become your follower; the second time for them to see your posts.

Even the solution of posting an inorganic and paid post straight away has its disadvantages. For instance, those Facebook users who agree to follow a business page do show a willingness for being provided with content. This is a valuable form of pre-qualification. Companies have, for good reason, mind you, a vested interest in targeting these very well-selected followers with high-quality content. Someone who might follow the brand Kitchen Aid on Facebook or Instagram identifies as someone being interested in high-quality kitchen appliances.

Clicks are more important than followers

Ultimately, companies are interested in attracting and directing their followers' attention, who, from a mere business perspective, are an open entry point to an interesting market potential. The aim here is to generate attention for products or other offers that are meant to be bought.

Clicks on your ad are particularly important, especially certain clicks, namely those on buttons like "More information," "Add to cart" or "Buy now." If users click (or tap with their fingers) on those, then you know that customers are explicitly interested in your content. The first and very important step has been taken!

With the seven-contact rule in mind, it becomes obvious that social media posts or advertisements are often early contact points in a sales process with (more or less) seven steps (Facebook and Instagram also have shops, but these are rarely a company's main sales channel).

Facebook, Instagram and such are very good at generating initial or general interest in a company and its products for potential sales. That is why clicks are often initially about precisely these processes – to generate or further interest. A "customer funnel" is then used to lead customers through various stages toward the purchase decision, most often to a website.

While considering this, companies should ask themselves how much such a click will cost them, this being one of the most important key performance indicators (so-called KPIs) for companies regarding their visibility.

KPI of the first order: CPC

The following illustration depicts these "costs per click" (CPC) based on typical types of social media advertising. It becomes clear that the value of such costs per click cannot be generalized for neither platform, advertising companies nor topic. Realistically, an expensive click is worth between 3 to 4 US dollars: on average, it is 1.72 dollars in the depicted sectors when companies use a somewhat functional campaign for exactly this goal. Here, customers are meant to be pre-qualified and made aware of the fact that they want to learn more, in order to then get them to click on the relevant button in a Facebook ad.

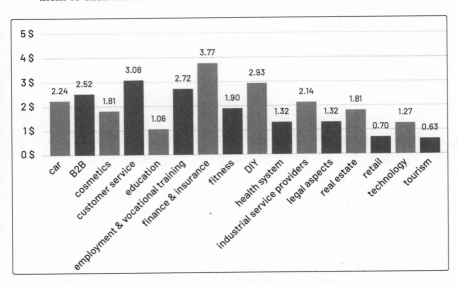

CPC prices on average for Facebook ads in US dollars. Depending on the topic, prices vary greatly.

Source: original illustration according to data from WordStream[3]

The reasons for the difference in CPC in different sectors is not easily explainable. However, assumptions can be made: if tourism, for instance, is characterized by a low CPC, this might probably be due to the fact that customers like to "drift" into, stumble upon this topic. The topic of traveling is a nice side activity. It is highly attractive to customers and they click frequently – without direct purchase intentions.

Finance, on the other hand, has a comparatively high CPC; it is directly economically attractive for advertisers because financial topics are lucrative. After all, customers are supposed to invest money here, thus, a lot of money is going around in these business models. Companies know this, and also know of the possible margins; they invest accordingly because the process promises a high return on invest if they manage a sale.

Moreover, as soon as a market is established as being lucrative, competition tends to also be strong. So, it is also about outdoing the competition with higher marketing budgets – driving up the CPC.

These are just two criteria that can be used to classify the different CPCs. They can be used to classify all other business models as well. Fitness, for instance, is very competitive but oftentimes has low margins, so the CPC tends to be low.

The rather small pillar of the real estate CPC raises another interesting question. Even though we can be sure of lively competition and high margins, the CPC is rather low with real estate. Obviously, there must be another factor at play that does not follow the study's logic. Presumably, the leap from attention for something on Facebook to a later house purchase – for many a high goal and a once-in-a-lifetime event – is too great. Therefore, real estate agents rarely see Facebook as a driving force for initial visibility.

Most importantly of all, the CPC needs to be measured for the company to then consider whether it is a realistic option for its marketing and whether it would show good results. The marketing channel is inappropriate when the CPC is very high, and the content is irrelevant for potential customers or the whole campaign was not fully optimized.

What makes the CPC so important anyway? The relevance criterion, thus, the most important dimension of smart visibility, which is fulfilled here with just one click: customers become aware of a Facebook ad only when it is relevant. Relevance turns a broad mass of potential addressees into interested customers. The CPC is the most important indicator of visibility with particularly high quality since no one clicks on uninteresting (i.e. irrelevant) content.

Therefore, CPC stands for relevance, and companies can measure it. If many potential customers click on an ad button due to the ad's or the content's visibility, then they are (measurably) expressing the topic's relevance for their very own customer need. This makes the CPC one of the most important KPIs for companies – not only for social media.

When customers click on an ad, it is like a little bell on a shop door. The door opens and a potential customer steps inside. It is an instructive metaphor since many aspects of the following process are similar to the workings of a sale in a shop. It is clear that the customer has a certain interest in the products, otherwise they would not have entered the shop.

Now it is just a matter of directing them.

Just as supermarkets make it difficult for customers to get to the till without having to pass vegetables, milk as well as many other products in many rows of shelves, you can direct your customers from that one click onwards.

You can also address them digitally on whether they need further information for their decision-making. Clever companies may be aware of the customers' frequent objections, some of which only make the decision-making process difficult for themselves. They then focus their marketing on such questions and suitable answers – before customers have even asked themselves (or the company) these questions: the so-called "anticipated objection."

This as well as several other processes that push the customer's purchase decision are put on excellent footing after the click because the relevance promise to the customer has already been fulfilled and they are now, with only a click, qualified as prospects with suitable needs. The ad has turned worthless visibility into a valuable visibility.

A company's entire marketing can be influenced by knowing the commensurability of the CPC. For one thing, it becomes clear that a determination of when this click happens is necessary because that is a clear indicator of the relevance promise fulfillment.

> The click parameter proves: communication with potential customers works! This means that the CPC is an important, measurable marketing goal.

Along this line of thought, reach marketing turns into performance marketing. Any kind of performance is always targeted because of a clear KPI, a targeted indicator.

Marketing that is measured in metric units can be reviewed and then optimized. This improves both customer communication and internal communication as well as goal achievement. "Our CPC has gone up" is much easier to check internally, and it is also easier to communicate when something is not going according to plan: "Somehow, our sales are down. Something is wrong with our marketing!"

KPI of the second order: CPL

Companies need to have detailed knowledge of the click and its costs because it is such an important indicator. Yet, companies do not do marketing for clicks, instead, it is just the first guided step in the sales process.

Traditionally, the next KPI is the CPL, the "cost per lead."

With retail businesses, do customers want to buy something right away or do they just want to browse and look around? The CPL describes the customer's desire for further information and contact; the digital equivalent being a lead. For instance, customers could leave their phone number or postal address for the shop to send them more information. Particularly, shops with high-priced items, such as jewelers or car dealerships, use this for the sending of high-value leaflets. The lead is an interim stage between the customers' first interest, setting foot in the shop and the later purchase.

Offline, the most likely place to see leads walking around is in car dealerships on a Saturday, out of unguided interest in cars or the brand and the new model, just browsing. After all, a traditional response to a salesperson wanting to direct the customer's interest: "I'm just browsing!"

Again, this is about maintaining contact. A clever salesperson would now encourage the customer to leave their business card. That, too, is a lead.

Since customers do not give one out lightly (after all, they just want to browse, with only a vague purchase intention), the salesperson has to help a little: they could offer the potential buyer a test drive, for which they would need to leave contact details.

However, this is more typical behavior in the digital world, with walk-in customers and random, brief encounters being transformed into directed interests. In retail or flower shops, no test drives are arranged, and customer data is rarely collected. This also depends on the product and the business model; processes with a longer consultation process have a greater need for leads.

With online-led processes of sales or prospect acquisition, many customers are much more skeptical because, among other things, some levels of communication are missing. With a salesperson in a shop, customers can communicate and build trust, which websites have more difficulty doing, thus, have to make up for this deficit. This is also the case in shops, but customers rarely leave contact info for shopkeepers to get back to them. In the digital realm, this is common practice: there, for instance, customers are asked to leave their email address for a newsletter mailing. Sometimes this is incentivized by a special offer of further information, a voucher or even an informative product for free.

Processes conducted online often require more contacts than those in a retail shop. While customers go to a shop and are very likely to decide for or against a product right then and there, in the online world, they can seek out more information, read test reports and make product comparisons with only a few clicks. They can first follow the product marketing on social media or sign up for a newsletter and gather more information.

From a business perspective, one aspect is particularly important that can also be transferred to the offline world: a lead, i.e. an opportunity to address the customer with information and advertising on your own initiative, is always valuable for companies. So-called "company doctors" who specialize in crisis management of troubled companies often ask during their audits how well the company can address its key network partners. This KPI of corporate certainty is often neglected by those companies. A reverse conclusion of this: active contact opportunities provide entrepreneurial security.

This does not only include suppliers and subcontractors but also customers. It makes a huge difference to many a company's success whether they can secure a communicative access to their customers. For digital communication processes, the lead is clearly another contact point with the customer and should be used first and foremost for an assurance of future contact points. Since customers do not buy many products at the first contact, it is a business responsibility to ensure as best as possible that further communication takes place.

Offline, shops do not think this far ahead and often rely on the logic of walk-in customers. They see customer interest as a process to which they react passively. Yet, the best advice is of no use if an insufficient number of customers take advantage of it or even hear about it.

That is the reason why companies – in both digital as well as offline communication processes – should consider their use of leads for the improvement of their own opportunities to address customers. They should provide them with information with their content marketing, thus, distinguish themselves from others as problem solvers. Such leads should be thought of as an opportunity for valuable visibility toward customers.

Companies can draw a "fence" around their most valuable customers, i.e. keeping them together. Yet, this only works to a limited extent if you build up followers on Facebook or other channels because these contacts are kept together "on rented ground": if Facebook blocks or suspends the company account, all access to the expensively built-up leads is lost.

Contact data, like a list of email addresses or telephone numbers, of your best (potential) customers, on the other hand, are corporate assets. These can also be funneled far more easily to even higher stages of the sales process.

KPI of the third order: CPS

The third, certainly a far from negligible KPI is the CPS ("cost per sale"). It describes the company's average costs for the realization of a sale.

Above all else, the CPS is the leading criterion. It is obvious that companies always have to measure their business processes regarding whether the return on investment was predicted correctly.

However, since our focus lies on visibility and marketing, we can reverse this logic: a check for a correct calculation of the ROI on every stage of visibility is not self-evident. Each individual step (CPC, CPL and CPS) must be equally measurable.

CPC and CPL are indispensable for the subsequent CPS. If visibility, which can be bought like any other commodity, does not lead to customers showing an initial interest, if there is no first click or if customers do not find their way into the shop, then this is a marketing bottleneck. If they then enter the salesroom with still no interest at heart, for instance, without leaving the contact info or without wanting to return, then this is the next bottleneck. If all these efforts ultimately do not lead to sales, then the bottleneck can be found here.

For an illustration of the individual stages: a company makes steel tools. A purchase of steel worth 100 euros is needed for the production of a tool worth 1,000 euros. This is economically sound. Now, though, an employee comes up with an idea for the company's own raw-steel production. However, because the company is inexperienced in this area and only needs small quantities of raw steel, production is expensive. Production, including the required amount of raw steel, costs the company well over 1,000 euros.

If the company now only calculates the market value of its own steel (it still being worth 100 euros), production seems to be economical. The mistake being: the company uses the wrong KPIs and overlooks sub-processes.

Similarly, companies need to look at preliminary stages of generating a sale to consider them on the basis of the KPIs (CPC, CLP and CPS) – as well as each separate sub-step.

Catalog of criteria for valuable visibility

Visibility is worthless when it ignores the three dimensions of visibility (relevance, authority, storytelling). This does not mean, though, that visibility is free of charge: visibility costs money, time and energy.

Companies know that they need to generate visibility for their products and services; if they do not know how to meaningfully convert this visibility into additional sales, they would rather, for good measure, generate *more* visibility than too little – from this, a learning curve emerges.

Google, YouTube, Facebook, the newspaper, the cinema or podcast platforms are channels of visibility and, in the short run, they do not care whether companies gain new customers either through advertising or less promotional content. Visibility on these channels for customer attention always costs advertising companies some money. Which is also what made Google and Facebook the highest valued companies in the world.

On the other hand, in the long run, platforms are very interested in companies gaining many customers through their channels, thus, remain motivated to invest marketing budgets. In case of doubt, it may just be sufficient that companies cannot know for sure whether it was this channel that brought them new customers or another. Maybe customers read about the product in the newspaper, which could then have motivated them to the purchase? Thus, further investment is done. This is not just whitewashing, but companies are flying their businesses blindly.

Still, it is tempting to create visibility on as many channels as possible. After all, this increases the probability of addressing the right customers with the right products at the right time – in other words, of gaining a new customer.

However, this is basically nothing else than a cross-channel escalation of scatter marketing. For instance, if you target a million cat owners with an advert about dog food on TV, you will sell very little dog food. This problem stays the same if you increase the scales, still reaching plenty of cat owners and a few dog owners also via radio, newspapers, podcasts and Instagram.

Poor or unsuccessful visibility scaled across multiple channels results primarily in *a lot* of poor visibility.

It may well be that changing channels can also bring a change to scatter marketing: perhaps the same customers are more likely to buy on a different channel. In fact, the same information presented on a different channel can appeal differently to customers, which might motivate them to buy.

Nevertheless, it would be better if – like a lottery ticket seller – you could draw the winnings right away and leave the rivets in the basket. Visibility and reach always cost money, so independent of your ROI, you need to install the KPIs CPC, CPL, CPS, on the basis of which visibility can then be assessed regarding its business benefit.

Channels differ in terms of cost, yield, the fit for one's company, its products, problem solutions and business goals. What could be a complete waste of money for one company could turn out to be the key to smart visibility for another. Decisions must be made and priorities be set.

This then results in a catalog of criteria for the generation of visibility. You should invest in it in a way that

- supports the three pillars of smart visibility;
- the visibility fits the product; for instance, products requiring explanation or are expensive need more visibility and in-depth content;
- reach pays interest accordingly, i.e. develops long-term effectiveness and continues or increases on its own;
- visibility allows for a good cost-benefit calculation;
- a clear goal is pursued, even if this cannot always follow the principle of "cause and effect" directly;
- the KPIs CPC, CPL and CPS can be collected and measured.

Companies tend to consider all channels for their marketing. However, they know that not all of them are equally suitable for their own requirements. They suspect or know that it would be far too time-consuming to actively use all, and that it would occupy important corporate resources. They also know that the costs for this much content, especially content marketing, would get completely out of hand. Still, they often cannot decide on the right strategy for each individual channel and across all channels. In companies, this creates uncertainty rather than optimism regarding their own visibility, or marketing is done on the basis of hope.

"Hope marketing," i.e. using many channels, usually uncontrolledly, hoping that individual marketing measures will lead to many business successes, or that the strategy will pan out somehow is actually a common practice. Yet, hope is no marketing plan! Companies should always ask themselves (at least, as best as possible): can we measure our own marketing success specifically and allocate it to certain visibility channels?

Short-term and long-term visibility

To meet the above-mentioned list of required criteria, we need to check whether our visibility has a long-term or short-term design.

The latter, for instance, is typical for Instagram. There, content or paid advertising continuously competes with other content. Users' attention windows are therefore relatively small. For users and senders of information, the end of the customer relationship is only a swipe away.

Mostly, it is sufficient to just observe yourself or someone else using Instagram, often as a sideline activity, for instance, during a train ride. This should give you, as an entrepreneur, a good insight into the forms of fleeting visibility you might be considering getting involved in.

A counter-example to this – i.e. long-term visibility – would be a podcast (which can last a good hour) or a book. Here, users devote more time to the offered contents, which are allowed to have more depth, and stringently follow the logic in which the narrator or author wants to pass on the content.

However, the access threshold to this customer attention, i.e. a higher level of visibility, is significantly larger. Is there anyone who always has the time for a whole podcast episode? Or who reads entire books on a topic?

Statistically, 57 percent of all German citizens have less than 50 books on their shelves.[4] So even this form of visibility is obviously of little use to companies if it is hard to achieve. Furthermore, not many companies can actually built stringent paths to their products with such a medium, like books or podcasts. What would James Bowen be trying to sell with *The World according to Bob*? Not cat food, probably. There is no distribution channel that results from a book.

With books, this stringent path to sales is cumbersome, at least if you think about it in the traditional way. Here, Instagram makes sense, where one billion global users give 3.5 billion likes a day, which means that every user gives attention to a certain information or product 3.5 times a day – making it countable.

Furthermore, an advertisement promoting a "buy now" button can easily be placed on Instagram: a clear and guided path between visibility, attention, interest and purchase, which takes place without a so-called "media discontinuity." This way, customers stick to their mobile phones or computers. That is less so with a book, maybe not even with a podcast.

However, Instagram's quick visibility, for instance, is there just as quickly as it is gone. If you put a professional in front of a reasonably set-up Facebook or Instagram advertising account, they will build you an ad in ten minutes that will reach tens of thousands of people within a day.

This ad, like an average post on Facebook, for instance, which can be compared to Instagram regarding its structure and usage, is only viewed for 1.7 seconds.[5]

A book, on the other hand, demands a lot from both author and reader. It is a significant time commitment to engage with this content. Truly, these two channels cannot be compared. At the same time, book content can have a completely different effect, unfold differently and bring more depth to a topic. It can replace several trust-building contact points between customers and providers. Customers can use a book to reassure themselves that the author knows what they are talking about and that they, if they also offer products and services, might be the right person to solve the customer's problem.

Still, books have far fewer chances of reaching a large number of people than Instagram. Plus, they have to be produced elaborately and with high stakes – will there actually be a willing publishing house for the finished, onerously written manuscript?

So which is the smarter channel: Instagram or books? Both forms of visibility have strategic and practical advantages and disadvantages. Which one makes more sense in individual cases: short-term, goal-oriented and high-energy visibility like Instagram, though it is encumbered by volatility, lack of content and interchangeability?

Or the book's long-term visibility, which takes a lot of effort to reach recipients?

Better still, use the strengths of one model to override the weaknesses of the other.

Used together, both forms bring it full circle

Short-term visibility is like a candy bar: full of energy, quick to consume and highly attractive. The energy in sugar is easily absorbed by the human body, but is just as quickly depleted again. This can be compared to an Instagram ad: viewed for seconds, understood right away, then forgotten if it cannot generate immediate relevance.

Long-chain carbohydrates, on the other hand, are a good metaphor for a book or a podcast, for instance. The body needs time to break them down, but it can also benefit longer from the contained energy which is available longer but at a lower level.

Facebook is perfectly capable of delivering clear information and advertising to customers quickly and accurately via a single paid ad. Potential customers then scroll through their Facebook feeds and come across the ad. This gives them a quick overview, on which they decide whether the matter is of interest to them. If you can built up relevance this way, the customers will give you a longer window of attention. And following said attention, they will want to get more information and give out a like – or, in a best-case scenario, even seek out a buyable solution for the described product. For this, they will check out the provider's social media channels or the given website.

From the marketing perspective, this is good, quick and energized.

For a mere Facebook ad, it does not make a difference whether the company's Facebook profile or its linked website provides high-quality information. Regarding its advertisements, Facebook is paid for the fact that customers become aware of advertisement, which is henceforth hopefully clicked on. This is all of Facebook's business model.

Facebook users, however, who just want to turn their freshly aroused attention into a purchase, do not care at all. That is due to the fact that this initial energy (i.e. attention) acts like the chocolate bar: if nothing follows the first impulse, then a "hypoglycaemia" of information, orientation and security follows. Customers' interests in the company's service flares up but finds only a bland hint to a possible purchase. Competing offers, information and the disappointed search for further guidance are the insulin peak that decreases the energy level again.

This means that good high-quality information needs to be added which, like carbohydrates, makes people feel fuller for longer, thus guiding customers through the process of gaining confidence and guidance toward the product.

A reference on the website, the social media profile or if the channel description to the book was published by a renowned publishing house or that the author has appeared in industry-renowned podcasts can give customers this security. Maybe this customer does not yet want to buy anything, maybe wants to read the book or listen to a comprehensive episode of the podcast first? This can give them the security for the product purchase.

Today's customers are well informed and definitely think about the supplier's side as well: not least from their fundamental skepticism toward promotional content, your customers intuitively know that claims in a Facebook ad cost little effort.

Yet, they also know that it takes far more effort to get a publisher to accept a book on the same topic and to then publish it. Or how work-intensive it is to create an elaborately designed website topic sound and coherently presenting on the same. References, testimonials and verifiable facts, a comprehensible structure and coherence of the abundant content support the customer's impression in both cases and generate long-term visibility.

They also know that a one-hour podcast provides them with much denser information than a briefly flickering Facebook ad.

Thus, there is no need for a book to counter the quick Instagram post – it is a good example though. Not least because its creation effort is extraordinarily high. It becomes clear that fast, agile marketing often goes hand in hand with little authority – and that building authority and trust (which work long-term) takes a lot of time and long wind.

Often, short-term and quick information such as Instagram posts or comparable marketing tools can take on a similar function as a book. They just need to be created and managed with a long-term effect in mind, which does make a clear difference.

If, for instance, customers visit a website via a Facebook or Instagram ad, and their short-term attention is to be transformed into long-term interest in the company and its products, a newsletter could help this process.

Therein, customers are not just offered purchases of a product but further information via this email newsletter. This is advantageous for both customers and supplier: customers continue to receive free information and (maybe even more importantly) further offers that strengthen their interest in a purchase – the supplier on the other hand gets the opportunity to give out a tolerable dose of exactly such guiding offers to customers.

Or even more directly: after seeing the promotional Instagram post, customers do not simply click on a link to the sales page but go to the company profile in the respective social media channel first or to the channel description on YouTube to get more information. Customers often want to know who is offering them information or advertising. There, content can shine in the long run as well.

At first, customers could just follow the company – a low-threshold option. They may want to receive regular information from the company, understand the product further and use the opportunity to slowly build trust.

This way, quick, energetic visibility can be transformed into long-term, permanently interesting visibility toward customers. If they agree to be repeatedly given small impulses, then this is also a long-term impact.

Incidentally, this idea also takes a phenomenon into account that can often be obsered with successful Instagram channels: particularly, influencers succeed in strongly binding their followers to this one channel with such fleetingly posted content. Despite the fact that contents posted there, both paid ("sponsored") and unpaid, evaporate just as quickly as any advertisement.

Still, there is essentially long-term commitment here by building up a basic offer of authority and good stories toward customers; from there, relevance can be developed in each case for the content and probably also for product offers down the line. This fulfills the three dimensions of smart visibility.

Thus, channels engage in good, long-term content marketing, which is highly relevant to their followers. Product offers can then benefit from this over-achievement in authority and storytelling.

Companies that are visible to their customers in a good and valuable way and use the three pillars of relevance, storytelling and authority well can intelligently use fast visibility for their business purposes. This then unfolds into special power and effect.

Whenever quick visibility suffers from missing authority as well as relevance and customers always suspect it of being overly promotional, a company can make good contact with them and make them a product offer with strong authority.

Customers know the company and its advantages as well as the qualities attached by them to the company's products from long visibility. In case of doubt, the relevance criterion is all that remains to get through to the customer.

It is then sufficient to give a small digital purchase impulse at the right time. Precisely this logic allows influencers to casually hold up a product into the camera and recommend it for a purchase. Something that quick print marketing, which is not further integrated into long-term visibility, would never be able to achieve, has a good chance of success here. This is why influencers sometimes get paid so well by companies just for their creation of visibility.

In sum, it is important to mix short-term and long-term visibility wisely. Both can usually be tracked well. Content and channels to which customers react positively are just as quickly found out as the ones that potential customers respond less to.

Retention or buying impulse?

Furthermore, companies need to decide whether they want to present content or marketing to their customers: content to bind customers or marketing to get them to buy something.

Of course, companies want to present marketing to their customers and guide them in a way that makes them willing to purchase something from them. The disadvantage: customers are often skeptical toward merely advertising contents. Which is why most companies could never again go without their content marketing department: customers are offered content free of charge in order to sensitize them for a certain topic or to emphasize the company's competence regarding said topic. This warrants the function of bond and guidance. Customers can be guided toward purchases on the basis of developing authority and good storytelling.

Between these opposing poles, loyalty and the buying impulse, a complex game of advertising and content unfolds, which is influenced individually by the market situation, customers, product and many other factors.

For instance, to support their own brand's stance toward customers, companies with a good market penetration produce spots that are less promotional and hardly call the customer to action. They want and have to maintain their market position because they can hardly conquer larger and fresh market shares. The brand itself even takes a back seat to the storytelling that conveys certain core values which they would want to see attached to the brand, and which rather creates or consolidates a sublime brand understanding in customers' minds.

Take Coca-Cola, for instance. It stands for youth and momentum, while Mercedes Benz does for dignified luxury. However, no concrete purchase invitation was ever formulated for either the lemonade or a special car model. The brand is visible without a clear buying impulse. Thus, the idea here is that customers will remember the brand which they like anyway – it just needs to be visible on a reasonably regular basis.

Other businesses use influencers to refer to the products without directly recommending a purchase.

In both forms of information design, a lot of content is created and a lot of loyalty is generated, but companies rarely give a clear impulse to buy.[6]

Organic or inorganic reach

The question of organic or inorganic contents is closely related to this complex interrelationship which is tied to posts on social media channels. Yet, it is less about the advertising parts of information sent out by companies, instead it needs deliberation whether the company will pay Facebook, Google and the like for the distribution of information – or whether it wants to use the free options for reach on its own digital business profiles and feeds.

Organic content is content on which a company or individual does not spend money for its distribution after having published it. For inorganic reach, on the other hand, platform operators get paid for the company to achieve certain visibility.

This distinction is common in social media and is also referred to as such; ultimately, though, there is organic and inorganic content in all media. In television, for instance, the series is the organic content and gets interrupted by the advertising blocks, the inorganic content. And here, too, there are mixed forms like so-called product placements in films and shows.

Customer retention and buying impulses play into this: at a TV station, content such as series, films, shows and news formats ultimately serve to retain viewers. And this retention, measured by viewer numbers, can then be sold to advertisers who want to trigger a buying impulse with their spots.

The advertising companies in TV formats like to use retention created by a lot of content which TV broadcasters produce for them. For this they pay with their commercial's broadcasting price.

Duoverse of visibility

This logic of inorganic and organic marketing, of retention and buying impulse, is particularly observable in the duoverse of Alphabet Google's and YouTube's parent company, and Meta the umbrella for Facebook, Instagram and WhatsApp.

With all platforms, companies have to decide how to position themselves in terms of content marketing and mere promotional content – and are aware of the consequences. YouTube is the biggest search engine for videos. Google's subsidiary firm offers the option of opening up one's own channel and of publishing original videos there. These videos are uploaded as organic content, thus, they are free of charge for everyone involved (both creator and user).

If these videos contain interesting information with more or less subtle hints at the possibility of buying the creator's products, then that is content marketing. This is also free of charge.

Still, no one has seen the video yet because no one knows about the new channel yet. With certain search keywords, which are either provided directly or in the video description, users can then find these videos. This works similarly to the well-known keyword usage with Google's search engine. Therefore, the visibility toward potential interested parties is accidental to a large extent.

The necessary luck can be helped along by paid inorganic content. For this purpose, videos are presented as advertisements before, during or after other videos. There is a close connection between content and marketing here as well, though promotional videos are now linked to other people's content, which is more or less convenient.

Google's search engine also works similarly. The primary sources of relevant content are websites – but YouTube videos as well as content from other providers such as rating platforms, blogs and ultimately even Facebook, Instagram and other platforms also play a role.

Content on the Internet is often presented on websites. Google goes through these, analyzes them for relevant content and presents corresponding search results to the platform's users. On the search results page, small snippets of the content that may be targeted then become visible to the person looking for something.

Website contents are therefore organic contents. If website operators want Google to give them preference to possibly millions of other search results, then this is done via paid advertisements: mostly, the first two or three hits on the list for many keywords are sponsored links.

Facebook can here be representative of the way Instagram works. Users generate a lot of organic content such as videos, texts or photos, which they then make visible to their friends and followers. Companies can do the same and show content to the people who follow them. In addition, inorganic content can also be created, so-called ads, which generate visibility beyond one's group of friends and followers.

With inorganic reach to new target groups

This means, organic reach has one big advantage: providers are not required to spend an advertising budget to achieve visibility toward potential customers. This is attractive for many providers; after all, a new target group can be reached with organic content and well thought-out content marketing. Yet, there are certain limits, which can then be overcome with inorganic content – needing a marketing budget.

For instance, one of these limits on Google is the fact that the probability of being listed on the first page of search results with one's website is anything but high. All search results that appear after the first page of the list are at a severe disadvantage and hardly visible.

Facebook also offers the option of buying visibility to gain new followers.

Companies hope that they will later be able to show these followers contents around the clock. After all, it is Facebook's inherent logic that followers see anything posted by their friends or the companies they follow in their feed. So what could be more obvious than using an increase of followers as a privileged key to organic, free and secure marketing? Unfortunately, the algorithm stands in the way of this.

Facebook cannot show all users all content that was put out there since so many users, companies, friends, institutions and advertisers produce content that competes with other producers of content and advertisements.

Thus, the algorithm sorts the content by relevance. If a Facebook user interacts with a company more often, sharing its contents and commenting on it, they will most probably and more frequently get to see more of that company's content.

Unfortunately, this probability can also be turned into the negative with similar criteria.

ROI of visibility is rarely ascertainable

The return on investment (ROI) of visibility has a business problem. It cannot always be ascertained because the path between investment and return is often very long. Most times, a budget for visibility can hardly be comprehensively allocated to a specific turnover.

In contrast, a sales representative in the field, preferably with a defined territory, can be matched to the effectiveness of their marketing measures with certainty. Since they are responsible for a certain region (for instance, a certain county), their salary and the company's other incurred costs can be offset against the turnover from contracts concluded in this area.

Either way, this only applies if the sales person gets the customers to sign contracts on the spot. Calculations become already more complex when customers (this can also be motivated by the sales person), for instance, go on the company's website, contacting the company through this channel.

And what about companies without sales people in the field, companies that use digital channels and analog promotional materials? What is a website's ROI and that of the other marketing tools?

Some make it possible to calculate that quite well. Take Facebook ads, for instance. Customers can be tracked there really well up to the point where they leave the shopping basket (the so-called "customer journey"), plus, it can also be tracked which expenditure was needed from the company to get customers there. These calculations of the ROI are far more difficult due to the scatter effect with other marketing measures like TV adverts or direct mail. Some companies want to manually track this by asking their customers upon contract closing: how did you hear about us/this offer?

Sometimes it is simply due to the seven-contact rule that it cannot be determined which contact point actually yielded a countable ROI and which ones did not. There is another flaw in the system: it is also impossible to know whether this contact point brought ROI but would not have without the previous contact points that then did not pull in this sale. Was it just the paid Facebook ad or had the customer known the company for a while through unpaid content on Facebook? What did the editorial creation of this content cost?

So, the ROI cannot always be measured. However, a warning against the wrong deduction must be issued: this does not mean that channels without a countable ROI or without a reliably attributable turnover can be neglected. In many cases, it is indispensable to take these channels into account – especially in regards to the seven-contact rule.

Often, visibility on Instagram cannot be attributed to an ROI any more than specialist articles in magazines, a trade fair presence or a customer event.

Therefore, the first approach should include the awareness of this challenge in one's own marketing, instead of simply devaluing individual channels. With most purchases, the customer will not have heard of the company or the product for the first time. A directly shortened ROI (visibility is immediately followed by a purchase) obscures the perspective on opportunities of smart visibility.

The second approach includes the presentation of a preferably very coherent message to customers on all the individual channels: what problem solution do company and product stand for? As soon as that is clear, it becomes less important where the first contact point was, but it increases the buying impulse with every further contact point, thus, decreasing the path to new turnover.

The third approach includes not being put off by the difficult or sometimes impossible allocation of sales to certain visibility channels. The use of all channels is necessary and equally important – but could be far too costly. Particularly smaller companies think that they do not have the time or budgets to aptly and simultaneously use a plethora of visibility channels.

On the one hand, channels can definitely be selected in regards to certain portfolio parameters. Some channels are better suited to a company, others less so. If your offer is geared more toward B2C customer relationships ("business to customer," i.e. end customers), then Instagram may be more of a channel for you. If you are more interested in B2B customer relationships ("business to business," i.e. corporate customers), LinkedIn may be the place to start with your visibility.

Think your content in kits

The content production for your visibility campaigns (like videos, illustrations, audio interviews, texts) is expensive. It is helpful to intensively exploit all the content you already have, i.e. to use it multiple times and across all channels. This way, every piece of content turns into a kit, a building set from which you can help yourself at any given point.

For the creation of content, interviews are conducted with exciting protagonists. These interviews can be filmed and later used several times for different channels. For instance, the video, originally produced for YouTube, can be used on Facebook and Instagram as well, the secondary channels. Or the video is made available to customers in a content area on your website, should they want to know more about the company and the product. On there, other high-quality content is also offered for critical and curious customers – supporting the reputation as a customer-friendly, honest and transparent company.

Particularly clear and strong statements from the finished longer videos can be cut out as individual "snippets" and be used for early customer contacts, for instance, as five-second advertising clips on Facebook. Customers expressing a clear interest in these statements – which Facebook can measure – can also be expected to "endure" more content in a second contact point, thus, shown the longer clip, combined with a link to the website.

Depending on the task, this would be a very sensible way to make use of the logic of the seven-contact rule. The short video snippet tests relevance, when this turns out positive, more interesting contact points can be offered.

This can be a very broadly thought-out game. Even a video's audio track can find a secondary use, especially when this other purpose was also considered during production. As a podcast episode via other channels for other customers, it becomes another contact point. The effort to extract an audio track as an MP3 from a video is very easily done, even for nonprofessionals.

This modular thinking, with kits in mind, which is only roughly highlighted here, can make a big difference in any marketing. Especially when it comes to the question of how to create visibility on many different channels, modular thinking is a disseminator of smart visibility. When particularly well-suited channels and content are chosen to find the perfect customers, which also have a good ratio of effort to visibility return, then even small companies can develop a competitive edge over the strongest competition.

In the following, you will find two tools that turn produced content into a sort of library that can be automatically displayed on various channels:

Canva: This online graphics tool enables even nonprofessionals to create very professionally looking graphics for a wide array of applications. Whether Facebook, Instagram, flyers, posters, website sliders or high-quality graphics for videos and presentations – Canva allows for elaborate and graphically balanced designs from ready-made templates. The templates are readily equipped with images and graphic elements as well as dummy fonts that only need appropriate replacements or a filling in.

Buffer: Buffer is one of several products that enable the production of social media posts as modular components. Just one morning for content production is enough for the preparation of several weeks or even months worth of social media content. Buffer then plays these out automatically according to a given schedule. The professional versions even allow for the statistics of individual post performances – otherwise, this has to be tracked in a more complex way by checking the channels directly. The most successful content can then be played out again. Customers rarely remember the specific content but rather its message. Companies can use this to their advantage by showing similar content several times. Here, redundancy is helpful because companies can show similar versions of a coherent brand image and the clearly formulated content again and again. After all, this content is relevant to customers and they will appreciate it accordingly.

Visibility as a resource is both plannable and an investment

Considering the common good of visibility as a resource, is a perspective guided only by the economical aspect. This also sheds light on a problem: usually, resources that are readily and abundantly available have a low market value. This was already pointed out earlier on. On the Internet, on hundreds of television channels and in thousands of magazines, on social media channels with millions of users, large amounts of content are constantly being produced that is more or less designed for a broad visibility.

Therefore, visibility is inflationary. For this reason, the abundantly available resource visibility must be refined to be able to find consumers (interested parties turned customers), be it through relevance, authority and storytelling. Visibility can – when refined – be an investment.

Therefore, an investment in the resource visibility must yield a return, which makes an examination of visibility regarding its potential return quite helpful.

Anyone who has ever dealt with equity investment will know that, when it comes to shares, it makes a difference whether you look at yield or dividend. A company issuing shares is selling shares in the company to investors. These have their advantages, for instance, the right to vote on certain business decisions but also the receipt of a share in the company's profits. If a company has done well in a year and made profits, it often pays out a dividend. This is calculated, though not directly, from the company's profits in relation to the shareholder's stake.

Particularly start-ups like to manage their business success according to this logic first – the so-called "performance-oriented" approach. All the company's actions are aimed at quick successes. It is about acquiring projects, completing them and finally invoicing for them. After all, start-up founders usually live off the running business, the "cash flow" – especially in the beginning. This operating profit then flows to the entrepreneur(s).

It is challenging to start one's own business and it is often also a hand-to-mouth business life for the entrepreneur(s), especially in the beginning: all investments are aimed at achieving the fastest possible cash flow.

All business successes are mopped up directly or used for necessary investments for further earnings. The first profits, for instance, go into renting an office, leasing a company car and commissioning the necessary website.

Particularly founders can hardly afford investments into their own brand, so they gamble on a later return or on future successes. With shares, though, that means: a share is bought and only possibly pays out a dividend. Even investors who know little about shares are informed on the fact that the share value can increase or decrease. This is closely linked to how the company runs things, how it performs in the markets and which business successes can be tracked.

Therein, shares are always also a gamble on the company. Its value often increases when it operates economically and favorable predictions for this business segment can be made. Yet, above all else, it helps when the company can integrate sustainable values which facilitate economic activity in the future.

The share prices could, for instance, increase when patents are integrated into the company or promising start-ups are acquired.

This line of thinking also works for smart visibility. Because investments in the company's future performance do not always turn out a dividend directly, i.e. a measurable profit. Still, they yield a chance of a long-term return – just like visibility.

An investment in your visibility costs money – like a company acquisition or a new development department would. They reduce cash flow, but they also promise a return in the medium run: as branding. At least, if they are managed well, expenditures to increase smart visibility can also increase the company value.

The brand becomes better known and increasingly more present to customers for certain well-defined core values and problem solutions. This is especially interesting because companies do not need to sell shares to get this return on visibility.

It was already described that a brand always adds some of its values for customers and makes those addressable for problems: "For problem X, I best turn to brand Y ..." This is a reversal from pressure marketing ("Did you know that we offer the following ...?") to pull marketing ("Can I get product X from you?"). This pull is created by a strong trust in the brand.

When customers know that a company can competently solve their problems, they will not need most of the gentle first contact points which are usually necessary for first-time customers. This decreases marketing costs and reduces the business effort, it creates a competitive edge and tends to allow for quicker growth – increasing profits.

Most start-ups cannot afford this luxury and investment; just as often, they do not think about it. Instead, they strive for contact points with their customers that lead to sales, if possible, even at first contact.

This leaves little room for branding, as the antithesis of performance-oriented visibility; at best, it is perceived as a pleasant windfall since the company would otherwise lose liquidity without a quick cash flow.

"We may not have closed a deal, but at least we handed out a few business cards" is a particularly dangerous motto for start-ups. Instead, business cards should not be seen as the primary goal, even later on, after the initial business success has been consolidated and it has now become a matter of also consolidating smart visibility with branding in mind. The brand needs to be charged in a way that it takes over establishing the company's visibility which would otherwise be expensive for every new customer contact.

"Brandformance" combines ROI and visibility

"Brandformance" combines a company's strive for a directly measurable ROI with the wish to build a good and radiating brand. In that word, the terms "branding" and "performance" are thought and their worlds brought together.

Marketing agencies think about this concept in technical and conceptual ways. Brands, for instance, will combine different concepts after maybe having established themselves in their markets, with enough budget on hand, now wanting to start in a new market.

There, TV spots explaining product benefits might be placed. At first, those would be shown on smaller TV channels because they generally are less expensive, plus, their audiences are considered to be more eager to buy. Viewers of pay-per-view channels or of teleshopping channels, for instance, have already proven with their choice in channels that they are willing to spend money. Thus, such marketing is aimed at cash flow: the spot is meant to be followed by measurable additional sales.

With these performance-oriented spots and channels, companies can grow quickly.

Only when this has proven successful, are TV spots broadcasted on TV stations with wider coverage. These tend to serve the purpose of brand recognition (so-called awareness) and are meant to primarily ensure that an increasing number of people beyond the special-interest channels hear about the brand and learn to associate something with it.

Ultimately, big brands like Coca-Cola or Mercedes Benz do the same: they rarely broadcast TV spots with clear intention for a call to action because they mostly have exhausted this potential already and have little room for growth. Often, the focus is not on a single product in these awareness spots. Instead, the brand defends its market position by getting lasting visibility and a stable charge of their brand with certain values. So the heart of the spot is "Mercedes Benz. Enter the new comfort zone" and not, for example, "Buy the new C-Class."

This is how some marketing agencies imagine brand performance; this reduces the idea behind it in which visibility is thought of as an investment in the value of one's own brand, and in which forms of visibility make a dividend possible and which ones may be expected to yield a long-term return.

Many business processes can invest this way in the brand without yielding a direct dividend. Customer events, an over-fulfillment of particularly good customers' orders or investments in the so-called social ROI[7], for instance with charitable commitments, are just a few examples.

Take writing a book, which can then be published by a renowned publishing house, or specialist articles which are then published in recognized periodicals – they cost time and even money in the form of opportunity costs: an author could start and manage processes that bring a much more direct turnover – instead of taking the time to write a book or specialist article and trying to come to terms with publishing houses.

Once a book like this is on the market, it becomes visible. With book sales and the author's fee, there is even a visibility dividend.

However, above all, specialist articles and books have a good visibility return, especially if they have been taken on by a publisher. It leads to visibility toward the target group and potential new customers. At the same time, a book, for instance, can replace business cards and generate high-quality visibility on a permanent basis: business cards are visibility items that are thrown away, lost or found in random pockets after months, having lost their content connection.

Business cards may build authority through professional titles, but they never convey stories to the same extent as a book does, and they could never in the same way support and convey the person's expertise whose name they bear.

Yet, books are rarely thrown away. Customers appreciate the renowned publisher and the book's visibility tool first. People have gotten used to truth, or at least carefully examined knowledge, in books and renowned periodicals in forever.

Therefore, books and specialist articles are levers of authority, thus, interesting for companies in terms of smart visibility. This form of visibility, as then occurs for book authors, for instance, pays interest, albeit, in the long run; this, too, is brandformance.

Book or specialist articles are vivid examples of how such a visibility return should be considered. Many other forms of visibility can trigger or support similar effects, and the same effects can be seen with podcasts of well-known podcasters in their chosen field.

Knowing the distinction between performance marketing and brand building should be an inspiration to all companies: the investment in smart visibility is working *on* the system, not *in* the system.

Channels of smart visibility

The previous chapter has proven that not all channels can be used and filled with content simultaneously. It does make sense to give preferential treatment to the channels with the best relevance KPIs (CPC, CPL and CPS).

Since companies cannot usually fill all visibility channels with content, it does make sense from a business perspective to decide which channels work best for the chosen purposes.

Which of the hundreds of channels make the most sense?

Instagram, Facebook, Google, Twitter, YouTube, Pinterest or TikTok – there are hundreds of different platforms that could be used as visibility channels.

For many companies, determining the best channels is a true challenge. Yet, what seems particularly confusing is on closer inspection in actuality quite manageable because companies can in principle assume that the basics of value-based visibility work similarly on all channels.

Even if one side of the equation (an almost unmanageable number of available visibility channels) is variable, the other side of the equation is very constant: potential customers.

Good storytelling, for instance, always works with customers – irrespective of medium and format. When a story offers contextual connecting factors and empathetic compatibility to customers, then a podcast, video or a series of Instagram posts can be used to tell of them. Which will probably work really well most of the time. When companies manage to establish relevance toward potential customers, to match product characteristics and customer needs as best as possible, then this is always powerful, independent of the chosen channel.

In contrast, the choice of channels for smart visibility is thus "only" an adjustment of the whole process.

Start with the most valuable channels

The following illustration shows two factors of smart visibility: the effort it costs to create marketing content or content marketing as a basis of one's visibility, as well as the potential use regarding one's own valuable visibility.

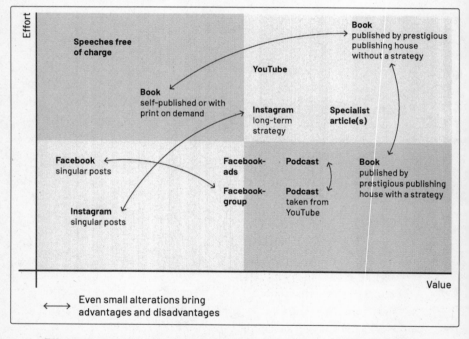

Effort and value of visibility channels are related to each other in different ways. The top left quadrant should be worked on last; here, there is no good proportion between effort and value. Whereas the lower right quadrant is particularly attractive. The arrows show that a channel's value can change with small alterations. This must be kept in mind during the implementation.

Source: original illustration

In addition, different corridors are drawn in the chart. In the quadrant with low effort at high value, a company should definitely consider the channels there. On the other hand, there is the quadrant with high effort and low value – this should be ignored completely or only be considered at a late marketing stage. This leaves two quadrants with a more complex relationship between effort and return on visibility.

Companies need to check these quadrants in detail since they cannot be classified clearly and must be considered individually regarding whether the effort would pay off measurably (via the KPIs CPC, CPL and CPS). The same, at least in principle, goes for the following: the assessment of how successful and with how much effort companies can generate visibility is individually different. It depends on the market and competition, on the products, the services, and on how much authority and storytelling can be developed for the product – to list just a few of the factors.

It is important and helpful to put effort and return in relation to each other – to then realize that you cannot simultaneously keep all balls in the air.

Furthermore, only some of the possible channels and tools of visibility are depicted here. The illustration is primarily about how to individually classify and then hierarchize visibility channels for a company.

Single Instagram posts are a good example of a visibility channel with low effort and usually also a low return. It offers customers few contact points and is also rather scarcely connected with other content. A typical example would be greeting one's followers on Instagram with: "Merry Christmas to all our customers!"

This post is created very quickly. A royalty-free picture of something Christmassy, like a tree, from one of the popular photo platforms and a remark, put together with a simple graphics program or directly in the Instagram app.

Yet, this content has no connection to the company at all and probably has a weaker effect on customer loyalty than the company would like to think. Instagram posts are stronger if they gradually build up good content and the associated power of persuasion, solidified into a convincing image for the customer with various arguments and content. If companies consider this and adhere to it, the evaluation of Instagram as a visibility channel already shifts in the illustration to more effort *and* more valuable visibility.

It costs a bit more effort to set up a Facebook post than a singular Instagram post, for instance. This is somewhat unexpected since the mechanisms are so similar. However, Facebook needs more text than Instagram, thus, more effort.

Followers make contact with the company's content via several contact points. One of these is the company profile, which can be filled extensively with content (company description and products, profile pictures and additional content) as well as references (links to the website, shop, Instagram, LinkedIn and an added mobile number for contact via WhatsApp, etc.).

The creation of an Instagram account with the few necessary pieces of information and first few posts is done comparatively fast because the app allows for far fewer contact points.

Additionally, in comparison, Facebook has less reach than Instagram: a smaller number of followers are shown a company's post. Thus, the effort's return on investment is simultaneously lower. From a business point of view, this makes Facebook much less attractive than Instagram.

However, again, this can be changed with a small alteration. Facebook groups, for instance, are a very high-value visibility contact point for many businesses. Providers can easily invite (potential) customers to it, be it for a certain topic, for discussions on it, for the publication of their own experiences and for them to be able to draw on group intelligence. The creation of such a group is done very quickly while the content itself, if managed well, comes almost entirely from (potential) customers; thus, only a small effort for the company.

Especially with topics of knowledgeable content (such as coaching, consulting, headhunting, engineering and science-related topics) and those that require a lot of emotional involvement from the fans, such groups are particularly well suited for customer retention. Without the company having to do much, while it can also even access the created content: what are typical customer topics that eventually show up in the discussions, thus, clearly referencing the pivotal aspect of relevance regarding customer needs? A good Facebook group can regularly answer this question.

This improves its reach because group members interact more with the content, which the Facebook algorithm then preferentially shows them. The content becomes more relevant and richer, while the necessary effort decreases.

There are other parts in the illustration where a similar relationship of a change due to few alterations can be seen. A book published by a prestigious publisher means a lot of effort. After all, this implies the writing of 200 or 300 pages of well-founded content. In return, the publishing house takes on the tasks of editing and checking, both in terms of content and style. As this is a very high obstacle, many authors take the other route of self-publishing their book or in the so-called "print-on-demand process." There, authors are their own editing authority, which enables them to quickly publish the book themselves. Yet, this not only lacks the publisher's marketing machinery, which gets the book into bookshops and online platforms (the latter of which is nearly impossible for self-published authors), it also lacks the radiating authority of the prestigious publisher. Readers recognize the publisher's work of checking and editing the book's contents, which implies that an author being published by such a publisher can deliver high-quality content. Being published by a prestigious publisher increases the book's perceived authority, which is in turn more useful for one's own valuable visibility.

Still, many authors underestimate this twofold shift between the quadrants in the illustration. A visibility tool with much effort and usually a high return on investment becomes weaker in relation to both values. Admittedly, it is easier to self-publish a book, but, in turn, it loses authority and its guidance function.

However, there are elements that show a particularly favorable relationship between both, podcasts being one of them. They are cheaply produced, especially when the sound can just be taken extracted from a YouTube video. Concurrently, you will have great influence on your listeners when it is distributed on popular platforms: podcasts are listened to at length, so that gives you the chance to compellingly present complex content and throw a light on an issue from different perspectives.

There is simply one problem with podcast: it has to compete against a vast number of competitors on platforms like Apple podcasts. Perhaps other forms of (quickly and easily implemented) visibility, like an Instagram post, can just as quickly and easily shore up visibility for the valuable podcast. Furthermore, the podcast which is perceived as a high-value format and which the Instagram post may point to, also irons out the latter's assumed weakness in content. Thus, a combination of different visibility elements can make a lot of sense, especially as the elements' advantages may cancel out the disadvantages, respectively.

When choosing one's own visibility channels, personal preferences can also play a role. One person may find it easy to produce videos for YouTube and get in front of a camera, while others might find it a great challenge. This changes the effort as well, even though the technical and content requirements remain the same.

Instagram: visibility is an easily accessed resource

Good news first: the systems of big providers like Meta (incl. Facebook, Instagram and WhatsApp) and Alphabet (incl. the brands Google and YouTube) are very easy to use. This makes it quite easy to become visible; moreover, KPIs help to test and compare these channels extensively.

The companies stand in direct competition to each other, which makes it easy for advertisers to buy visibility. Obviously, you could also book social media agencies, but nothing speaks against taking the first steps toward visibility by yourself. These providers have long since realized that they have to make low-threshold offers to companies with their marketing budget. This makes it easy for niche companies to get a lot of visibility in their field for only a small budget (10 pounds a day might just be enough to reach 5,000 to 13,000 potential customers on Instagram who might be interested in just the product you are trying to sell).

Albeit, campaigns with much larger budgets should really be managed by professionals, like social media agencies, or by the particular department in the company.

By the way, this concept works on nearly all social media channels: high-quality and good visibility can be bought for the absolutely relevant target group.

Your YouTube channel

YouTube is one of Google's subsidiaries and, just as Google is the largest search engine for web content, YouTube is the world's largest search engine specifically for videos. It has around two billion users worldwide who use its content at least once a month, one billion of whom watch videos daily. At the same time, 90 percent of all people between the ages of 18 and 44 with access to the Internet have used YouTube – this is a large share of the so-called "advertising-relevant target group" (the age group 14 to 49 is considered to be particularly eager to buy, thus, interesting for businesses).

This means that YouTube's content has easy access to the Internet users' attention. Therefore, it is particularly recommendable as a visibility channel. This is also due to the fact that YouTube specializes in highly relevant content. For many users, video content is a notably popular source of information. On the one hand, YouTube can be used for trivial entertainment or as a so-called "second screen," on the other hand, it can help aggregate a lot of information in a short amount of time.

The possibilities of audio-visual depictions have many advantages: illustrations can be used just as much as elaborate video animations; real images and tables can be combined; cinema-quality advertising can be produced or very authentic home videos can be made – the possibilities of visual depictions are manifold. Furthermore, for a second level of information transfer and emotional reinforcement, auditory content can be added, like a narrator, original sounds or even a professional score.

Videos have another advantage still – especially in regards to a company's customer approach. It is basic psychology that people tend to trust other people when they can look them in the eye. Unconsciously, people are convinced that the more sources of communication (such as gestures, facial expressions and other behavior by the person opposite) they have at their disposal, the better they can check for authenticity and honesty. Since both are important pillars of authentic marketing, video as a medium can also take on interesting functions here.

Often, new media or new formats and forms of broadcasting can have an influence on an entire field's content. For instance, music videos in the 1980s and 1990s, with their special styles, fast cuts, bright colors and imaginative presentations on known music channels (a leading medium of youth culture), were a great influence on how television formats and cinema films were subsequently edited.

Similarly, the ability for almost anyone to publish videos has influenced the reception of the whole medium. Thus, a certain imperfection is not only accepted but is even perceived as a particular indicator of authenticity. Videos and also their users (if they are not suspected of being paid by large corporations, but express their opinions without bias) carry this claim of independence and authenticity. This not only influences the fact that viewers of such videos, especially on YouTube, like to use these sources, it also influences the acceptable video quality. Whereas the quality of television productions used to be the benchmark, shaky camera work, average sound and a few slips of the tongue are now almost a distinguishing element of credible content.

Your own podcast

In comparison to other media channels, podcasts have more depth regarding its content. Listeners often spend half an hour or even an entire hour on a podcast. For providers, this has the advantage that they can present very detailed and well-founded content. They can circumvent many of a commercial's challenges in terms of getting viewers' attention.

Podcasts can cleverly convey a high degree of good arguments, examine counter-arguments and give honest insights into an issue.

41 percent of Americans[1] listen to podcasts regularly, the majority of which at least once a month. Apple, for instance, offers its users its own podcast app as a special adaptation to the increasingly mobile use of podcasts. 74 percent listen to podcasts on their phone and podcasts are often a kind of accompanying medium that listeners can follow well while doing something else like driving or housework. Therefore, they are happy to consume longer content on one topic. At the same time, Apple users are considered to be especially keen on buying, which increases the chances of advertising successes. Podcasts also have practi-

cal advantages: they can be developed together with a YouTube video. Free video editing software allows everyone to easily extract the audio from a self-produced video and to upload it as a podcast. With just a little bit of planning but little effort, high-quality contents can be presented to potential customers on several channels.

Podcasts are also a very good medium to present a talk between two people, for instance. Therein, scrutinized knowledge and different opinions can come together here. Companies can choose whether they invite an expert to their podcast episode or send one of their own to someone else's.

Email marketing has the highest added value

Your (potential) customers' email addresses can be your most valuable asset. Emails seem almost antiquated against the backdrop of many social media channels which appear more current. Yet even today, the ROI of an email campaign is extraordinarily high: for every invested euro in email marketing, companies can earn up to 42 euros. Even to this day, this value increases regularly due to the channel's increasing professionalization. Since the last time he checked, the study author found out that the revenue, for instance, had increased by 10 euros for every 1 euro invested.[2]

Emails have advantages in the subsequent automation and efficient addressing of many customers. Telephone numbers, for instance, are also customer data and can be used for acquisition purposes; however, the potential customers need to be approached individually – a much more time-consuming endeavor.

It should be taken into account that companies who want to address a few thousand potential customers only need to write one initial welcome email and two or three follow-up ones. It is time well spent, when it takes just one day of building a tested and optimized process for perhaps 1,000 email recipients.

However, email marketing has more strategic advantages than just that which make it one of the best systems for valuable business visibility. For one thing, it has the great advantage over Facebook, LinkedIn or YouTube that contacts with one's own (potential) customers are not made and saved on "rented ground." Instagram is only the platform which provides the possibility to show organic posts to followers of a company page or a personal profile – but it always remains an intermediary. Although users interact with the companies' content and advertising, they are and will always be solely customers or members of Instagram – which also applies to all other social media platforms, of course.

As was already pointed out, the quota of organically displayed content is also very low. At this point, a well-maintained email list from a renowned provider of email marketing automation, who takes care of guaranteed delivery rates with also low spam rates, works much better.

Now, Facebook's poor delivery rates for content can certainly be compensated for. For this, ads are placed that are then shown to followers, thus, achieving a delivery rate of almost 100 percent. This is not linked with any costs in an email marketing system – which it very much is with Facebook, due to the given advertising budget.

This means that email marketing only incurs costs once: an email list – analogous to followers on social media – must be built up. So, these initial costs and the effort of a recipient list have to be paid either way. However, sending further content to these recipients is free of charge after the initial costs.

Emails also have a higher chance of success reaching customers. On the one hand, this is due to the other (advertising) content on Facebook or Instagram, for instance, which it always has to strongly compete with. This becomes obvious as soon as we check our own phones and see such content in the feed right next to other colorful, content-rich and interesting content – to everyone's chagrin since all content has to share the available attention.

Emails, on the other hand, usually have quantitatively less competition; hardly anyone gets as many emails a day as they see posts on their Instagram feed. Above all, this content also has a different quality – especially when you manage to collect emails from the same business backgrounds. Then, an email from one sender is in best company with other important, professionally and personally relevant content. As soon as your customer opens an email, you have their undivided attention – at least, as soon as you manage to stand out from the flood of spam in their inbox.

Thus, you need to ensure that you create relevance for customers as early as the subject line.

A good email address list ensures this relevance by pre-qualifying customers. For instance, you collect the emails with a high-quality squeeze page. This refers to websites on which customers' email addresses are collected in exchange for valuable information which companies offer them. This, in a sense, provides a "working sample" of the company's possible relevance promise.

Here, companies prove to customers that they are good at formulating and solving problems and needs: the definition of relevance. Ideally, the information material sent can then build the other important pillars of value-based visibility, especially authority and storytelling, and thus pre-qualify the customer for further interesting offers. Often, even a small but well-maintained list of email recipients can make a big difference, even regarding hard sales targets. Thanks to powerful systems, the technology for email marketing is easy to master today.

Webinars qualify the lead and lead to sales

Webinars are digitally led seminars, which can be done live with a facilitator. This has one disadvantage, though: the facilitator needs to be present at the time of the webinar. With ever new prospective participants, this live webinar has to be organized several times a week – this costs resources and hours of work.

This problem can be avoided with being a bit clever and recording the webinar the first time, for it to then be shown to the interested participants. A strong-selling webinar familiarizes the participants with the product, the webinar content should be designed along the lines of the pillars of smart visibility to give participants an understanding of the product's relevance. A valuable webinar can also build up the producer's authority and tell a good attention-grabbing story.

The webinar should finish with a clear call to action with an offer of purchase.

Your own website automates sales

Your own website is your "marketing mothership." Companies often think of this visibility tool when asked about digital visibility – justifiably so. Websites are the central online contact point for (potential) customers. This begins at the short info on a shop's opening hours – one of the most searched information on the Internet – and goes on with a deeper search of a company's portfolio, references and testimonials. Sometimes, customers check the website in much detail for indicators whether the company's initial visibility or an initial idea of a product promise aligns with their individual customer needs.

Particularly a website can convert visibility to revenue, and it is oftentimes much better at this than most other elements of visibility. On Facebook or Instagram, the last move to a customer purchase is often either through arguments or through customer retention not sufficiently prepared – or simply impossible from a technical perspective.

Furthermore, a website does not assume a media break regarding many processes. When a potential customer is reading a book or listening to a podcast, they cannot buy a product from the company through these. They have to find another way and show the necessary initiative. From a marketing perspective, this is always a pitfall for selling processes.

Such a selling process can be established on a website through a shop or the link to an online sales platform much better. In addition, the process of matching customer needs with the product promise has to be carried out in greater depth than in many media preceding the seven-contact rule.

Depending on product and previous customer acquisition, the website can be an interface to further processes of contact with customers. For instance, it can invite customers to subscribe to the newsletter or, depending on product and previous customer acquisition, it can be an interface to further sales processes.

Your own sales funnel made of system modules

With the elements shown here, it is possible to build your own sales funnel without any knowledge about technology or marketing – because system providers take care of that.

A traditional funnel starts with the components of guided, high-quality visibility – regardless of the selected channels. Here, the CPC parameter is determined and evaluated. In the next step, website visitors become leads when the customer hands over their email address to then receive, for instance, a digital info product. The resulting CPL is also tracked.

Via the newsletter, an invitation for a webinar is sent to customers, which can be shown to them fully automatized.

The process is finalized with the turnover from smart visibility. For this, the product is sold to customers directly through the webinar; should they not take on this offer, there will be a follow-up email. At this point, the CPS is tracked as a separate KPI.

Acknowledgments

A book like this rests on many people's shoulders, people who have accompanied me for years.

I would especially like to thank my co-author Jan Bargfrede, who condensed my content into this book and patiently and highly professionally invested many months in this project.

My personal thanks for their many years of support far beyond this book go to Stefanie Sommerfeld (personal assistant) and Riana Machoy (graphic designer and social media professional).

For years, I have been friends with many of my fellow Internet founders. I would especially like to thank Julien Backhaus, Pascal Feyh, Mike Hager, Thomas Klussmann, Sven Platte, Bodo Schäfer, Hermann Scherer, Ralf Schmitz, Mario Wolosz and the 30 entrepreneurs in my annual Weissenhaus Mastermind Circle.

With a high degree of sympathy, I would like to thank Joachim Bischofs (Campus) for his many years of familiarizing me with the international book market, his quick troubleshooting at the publishing house and for his cooperation on my books – often during his free time.

I would like to thank my editor Patrik Ludwig for his extremely pleasant, very professional and, what is more, timely feedback on this book. I would also like to thank Georg Hodolitsch (FBV) for his constant support.

I thank the following people for their many years (often, decades) of inspiration and friendship:

Markus Fatalin, Dr. Carsten Figge, Dr. Andreas Gekle, Andy Goldstein, Alexander Kröger, Norbert Leibold, Prof. Dr. Bernhard Lendermann, Dr. Lutz Mahlke, Prof. Dr. Friedrich Meyer, Prof. Dr. Stefan

Nieland, Prof. Dr. Carsten Padberg, Dr. André Pott, Dr. Gerhard Sandmann, Jörg Schieb, Jan Schust, Dr. Andreas Siebe and Prof. Dr. Thomas Werner.

I also want to thank my parents Margot and Werner as well as Daniela Lena, Anna Carina, Finn Jonas and Emily Johanna for being my home.

Prof. Dr. Oliver Pott

Paderborn and Weissenhaus, Germany

Endnotes

Invisibility equals nonexistence

1   https://www.scientific-economics.com/der-primacy-recency-effekt-aus-der wirtschaftspsychologie/, retrieved: 05 January 2022.
2   https://de.wikipedia.org/wiki/Halo-Effekt, retrieved: 05 February 2022.

Be visible – and find the best customers and make more sales

1   https://www.insider.com/instagrammer-arii-2-million-followers-cannot-sell-36-t-shirts-2019-5, retrieved 05 January 2022.
2   https://www.futurebiz.de/artikel/youtube-statistiken/, retrieved: 05 January 2022.
3   https://blog.hubspot.de/marketing/google-trends-suche, retrieved: 05 January 2022.
4   https://allfacebook.de/toll/state-of-facebook, retrieved: 27 October 2021.
5   https://www.futurebiz.de/artikel/aufmerksamkeitspanne-facebook-mobil/, retrieved: 03 November 2021.
6   Translator's note: "Geiz ist geil!" and "Ich bin doch nicht blöd!" were famous and (from a pop cultural perspective) popular phrases coined by the German electrical retailers Saturn and Media Markt, respectively (now part of the same company) – the slogans of which were literally shouted at consumers to drive the point home.
7   Easton Ellis, Bret: *White*, Picador 2020.
8   https://blog.ppstudios.de/2018/08/09/was-kuenstler-noch-an-ihrer-musik-verdienen/, retrieved: 20 January 2022.
9   https://en.wikipedia.org/wiki/Long_tail, retrieved: 13 September 2022.
10 Translator's note: the British version of which was *You bet!*
11 https://www.rolandberger.com/de/Insights/Publications/Lineares-Fernsehen verliert-weiter-an-Bedeutung.html, retrieved: 25 January 2022.
12 *DIE WELT*, 25 January 2022, p. 16 [in German].
13 https://www.oetker-verlag.de/buecher/dr-oetker-schulkochbuch/, retrieved: 24 January 2022.
14 https://medium.com/cuepoint/jennifer-paige-what-ever-happened-to-me-858b29da95be, retrieved: 24 January 2022.

15 https://www.tagesschau.de/wirtschaft/unternehmen/k-pop-musikindus trie-101.html, retrieved: 24 January 2022.
16 https://www.zeit.de/digital/2021-03/tiktok-social-media-plattform-pop-musik-charts-musikindustrie?utm_referrer=https%3A%2F%2Fwww.google.com%2F, retrieved: 25 January 2022.
17 https://www.mpib-berlin.mpg.de/pressemeldungen/informationsflut-senktauf merksamkeitsspanne, retrieved: 25 January 2022.
18 https://dl.motamem.org/microsoft-attention-spans-research-report.pdf, retrieved: 24 January 2022.
19 https://www.bonedo.de/artikel/einzelansicht/darum-werden-popsongs-im mer-kuerzer-aufmerksamkeitsspanne-sinkt-um-ein-drittel.html, retrieved: 26 January 2022.
20 Here, the scientific theory behind it is simplified and generalized. Obviously, the cited (German) study goes far more into detail than the point made here: https://www.bwl.uni-mannheim.de/media/Einrichtungen/imu/Research_Insights/2016/RI_042.pdf, retrieved: 09 October 2021.
21 Roughly based on *Gabler Wirtschaftslexikon*.
22 https://de.wikipedia.org/wiki/K%C3%A4se, retrieved: 09 October 2021.
23 https://www.feinschmecker.com/artikel/franzoesische-kaese-handwerk-aus-dem-kloster/, retrieved: 05 January 2022.
24 Translator's note: Demeter is a German organic farming association whose members practise biodynamic agriculture based on the agricultural concepts and the spiritual-esoteric worldview of Rudolf Steiner's anthroposophy.
25 Here, we do not use the quality connotation in its economic sense: quality is the fulfillment of the customer's expectations. So, if it is the customer's main expectation to be able to quickly prepare cheese sandwiches for three children in the morning, than pre-sliced, industrial cheese has a clear qualitative edge to hand-made cheese.
26 Translator's note: known as "Lynx" in some parts of the world.
27 https://www.youtube.com/watch?v=RBA_o4qloXk, retrieved: 6 September 2022.
28 https://www.youtube.com/watch?v=-6IMOd5yI-I, a German ad from the car manufacturer Opel, 1975, retrieved: 05 January 2022.
29 Translator's note: German food company for cereals and bars, etc.
30 Translator's note: a well-known brand of dental care products in German-speaking countries, especially toothbrushes. Best known for the claim that "the more intelligent toothbrush yields."
31 https://www.youtube.com/watch?v=dvMqG8sbTtw, an ad from the German brand "Dr. Best," retrieved: 05 January 2022.
32 https://www.youtube.com/watch?v=dvMqG8sbTtw, an ad from the German brand "Perlweiss" (engl. pearlwhite), retrieved: 03 November 2021.
33 https://www.researchgate.net/profile/Wolfgang-Schweiger/publication/273922 576_Was_bringen_prominente_Testimonials_-_Werbewirkungsstudien_in_ der_Meta-Analyse/links/5a549e2ca6fdccf3e2e2f2df/Was-bringenpromi nente-Testimonials-Werbewirkungsstudien-in-der-Meta-Analyse.pdf, retrieved: 05 January 2022.
34 https://www.absatzwirtschaft.de/die-studien-der-woche-empfehlungsmarke

ting-einzelhandel-versus-internet-und-der-smart-tv-trend-68011/, retrieved: 05 January 2022.

35 https://www.brigitte.de/mode/trends/chiara-ferragni---co---das-sind-die-er folgreichsten-influencer-der-welt-10967484.html, retrieved: 03 November 2021.

The three dimensions of valuable visibility

1 https://www.wirtschaftspsychologie-aktuell.de/magazin/facebook-kennt-dich-besser-als-deine-freunde/32/, retrieved: 18 October 2021 [in German].

2 https://www.researchgate.net/figure/Fuente-Newspaper-Association-of-Ame rica_fig1_296419858, retrieved: 25 January 2022.

3 https://www.swr3.de/aktuell/nachrichten/banksy-auktion-rekord-100.html, re-trieved: 14 December 2021.

4 Based roughly on an article published in the German newspaper *DIE WELT*, in which a professor of art history is being cited: https://www.welt.de/debatte/ kommentare/article123985985/Das-Geschaeft-mit-der-abstrakten-Kunst.html, retrieved: 13 December 2021.

5 A small test in this regard: try playing the well-known game of "I packed my bag ..." with this method. Put down the pieces like tooth brush, life preserver and diving goggles along a route that you can track well in your mind, maybe because you walk it daily. The more offbeat the location and the more impressive the pictures (diving goggles on a door knob, flippers in the letter box), the better this mental journey will work.

6 https://www.ihk-akademie.de/kurs/2425/story-telling-marketing-nicht-nur-fuer-die-grossen/, retrieved: 05 December 2021.

7 https://onlinebusinessakademie.net/verrueckte-geschaeftsideen/, retrieved: 09 December2021.

8 https://www.bbc.co.uk/programmes/b00snr0w.

9 https://www.youtube.com/watch?v=V6-0kYhqoRo, retrieved: 27 November 2021.

10 As an example for German crime television, only two cases in the long-standing *Tatort* series were kept unsolved: https://www.handelsblatt.com/arts_und_ style/lifestyle/tv-film/tatort-statistik-nur-zwei-todesfaelle-blieben-ungeklaert/ 20792250-2.html?ticket=ST-2757623-ZfmtTmdFQ5MfPHDucRhV-cas01.ex ample.org, retrieved: 17 January 2022.

11 https://www.youtube.com/watch?v=S5bZ5byXjEM, retrieved: 28 September 2022.

12 https://www.auto-motor-und-sport.de/verkehr/consumer-report-usa-2021-ele ktroauto-studie-tesla-audi-porsche/, retrieved: 26 November2021.

13 Sinek, Simon: *Find your why: The practical guide to discovering purpose for you or your team*, Portfolio 2017.

The six levels of smart visibility

1 Godin, Seth: *Permission Marketing: Turning Strangers Into Friends And Friends Into Customers*, Simon & Schuster 1999.

2 According to the German Federal Office of Statistics: https://de.statista.com/

statistik/daten/studie/446308/umfrage/spam-anteil-weltweit-in-unternehmen/, retrieved: 05 January2022.

3 Translator's note: a German career-oriented social networking site that has been on the market since the early 2000s.

4 https://speed-ville.de/peloton-bike-test/, retrieved: 05 January 2022.

Directed visibility equals turnover

1 https://de.statista.com/statistik/daten/studie/788266/umfrage/online-besu cherzahlen-von-jameda-als-zeitreihe/, retrieved: 05 January 2022.

2 https://blog.fanpagekarma.com/de/2019/03/05/was-man-von-stories-erwarten-kann/ [in German], retrieved: 25 January 2022.

3 https://www.wordstream.com/blog/ws/2017/02/28/facebook-advertisingbench marks, retrieved: 25 January 2022.

4 https://de.statista.com/statistik/daten/studie/71160/umfrage/anzahl-der-bue cher-pro-haushalt-im-jahr-2008/ [in German], retrieved: 28 December 2021 – we accept the older statistic here since these values probably fluctuate little.

5 https://www.futurebiz.de/artikel/aufmerksamkeitspanne-facebook-mobil/, retrieved: 29 December 2021.

6 Influencers do actually formulate a "Call to Action," though this is not predetermined by the companies. This does make a difference regarding the separation between content and marketing.

7 The SROI (Social Return on Investment) was created as a KPI to also be able to rate the success of companies which are not primarily construed for profit like companies with a social economical or charitable purpose. In a wider definition, however, commercially oriented companies can also convert social ROI into monetary profits, for instance by increasing visibility or by linking it to certain social values.

Channels of smart visibility

1 https://de.statista.com/statistik/daten/studie/1266148/umfrage/podcasthoer erschaft-in-den-usa/retrieved: 17 January 2022.

2 https://dma.org.uk/uploads/misc/marketers-email-tracker-2019.pdf, retrieved: 17 January 2022.